Given Up for You

LIVING OUT

Gay and Lesbian Autobiographies

David Bergman, Joan Larkin, and Raphael Kadushin
FOUNDING EDITORS

Given Up for You

A Memoir of Love, Belonging, and Belief

Erin O. White

THE UNIVERSITY OF WISCONSIN PRESS

The University of Wisconsin Press
1930 Monroe Street, 3rd Floor
Madison, Wisconsin 53711-2059
uwpress.wisc.edu

3 Henrietta Street, Covent Garden
London WCE 8LU, United Kingdom
eurospanbookstore.com

Printed in the United States of America

This book may be available in a digital edition.

Library of Congress Cataloging-in-Publication Data

Names: White, Erin O., author.
Title: Given up for you: a memoir of love, belonging, and belief / Erin O. White.
Other titles: Living out.
Description: Madison, Wisconsin: The University of Wisconsin Press, [2018]
| Series: Living out: gay and lesbian autobiographies
Identifiers: LCCN 2017042903 | ISBN 9780299318208 (cloth: alk. paper)
Subjects: LCSH: White, Erin O. | Lesbian authors—United States—Biography.
Classification: LCC PS3623.H5747 Z46 2018 | DDC 813/.6 [B]—dc23
LC record available at https://lccn.loc.gov/2017042903

This book is a work of memory. I have tried to re-create events and conversations as
they occurred, but surely have not done so with complete accuracy. The names of some
individuals have been changed to protect their privacy.

For **CMC**

Contents

Given Up for You

1 | The Dinner Party

It was eight o'clock and everyone at the party wanted to know where she was. "She's running," Jen said when one person and then another came into the kitchen to ask for Chris, who was, I quickly gathered, the guest of honor. Chris was always running in those days, although I didn't know that then; I didn't yet know anything about her. Later I would learn she often ran for two or three hours, and on hot nights like the one of the party she set out in the cooling dusk and ran until long after dark.

She finally arrived just before nine, wearing cutoff jeans and a white T-shirt, her short blonde hair still wet from the shower. From the kitchen I heard a loud welcome and then a chorus of teasing for her lateness, and even from where I stood at the counter, slicing baguettes and trying to appear as though I belonged, I could see the teasing was a beloved ritual; they had been waiting on her for years and—running or no running—they would wait again.

"She's been in New York," Jen said, motioning to the porch with her paring knife, "but she joined a Philly firm last month, and she's back in the neighborhood." She reached for a beer bottle and took off the cap. "Let's bring her a beer," she said, "and I'll introduce you." I followed Jen out to the porch. She held open her arms, then stepped back. "Is that shower or sweat?" Jen asked. Chris didn't answer, only took the beer bottle and walked into the embrace.

"I'm Chris," she said as she pulled away from Jen and turned toward me. She put out her hand and smiled at me in a way that seemed to turn her eyes into small suns, the skin around them folding into thin rays. She was taller than me and her hand was strong; I could see the muscles in her tan arms, in her shoulders. She wore a red string around her wrist, and when I looked down I saw that she wasn't wearing any shoes. I didn't understand how it was possible for someone who looked like her to be a lawyer.

I had been invited to the party to meet a man. The man was a poet, and he was quick-witted and wiry in the way of many poets I would later meet. The introduction was a kind gesture on Jen's part, the sort of thing a married woman did for a friend who had, at the tender age of twenty-three, broken up with her live-in boyfriend and moved to a downtown studio apartment. I was lonely in those days, although I didn't recognize what I felt as loneliness. I thought I was just becoming an adult.

Eventually we all made our way to the table. I sat next to the poet and across from Chris. There was a toast to her return and she inadvertently drank from my wineglass. I toasted her with water, and when she turned away I took back my wineglass and emptied it in one long swallow.

Later Jen would tell me if she had known about me she wouldn't have bothered with the poet. I told her not to worry. What I didn't say was how could you have known when I barely knew myself? I only dated men, only sought men. But I noticed women. Occasionally I would meet a woman and her hand would linger against my palm when we were introduced, her gaze would seek mine at the table. I came to understand the wordless, daring question she was asking me: *Am I right?* I learned to answer with my own lingering hand, my own glance away and back again: *Yes, yes, you are.* And although I learned to not be afraid of my wanting, I also did not act on it. I turned away, I took back my hand; I waved my good-byes from the door. I wasn't interested in what came next. My desire was simply too quick to cool. It was moody and adolescent, but because I was not an adolescent I didn't let myself begin something I couldn't keep aloft.

Which is why I did not expect what happened at the dinner party. I did not expect that the flicker of wanting I felt at the sight of Chris on the porch would not fade, and that I would, again and again over the hours of the party, meet her gaze and seek her attention, pass her bowls of food and keep my hand on them too long, waiting for her hand to press against mine. That night I felt my desire bloom heavier than it ever had before, which had the mysterious and miraculous effect of allowing me to see her desire, to see her watch me and speak to me in a way she was not watching or speaking to anyone else.

When it was late and I had clearly missed the last train back to the city, someone at the table said something to Chris about a girl and Chris smiled and took a long drink from her beer bottle. And I knew then what I could do—what I could make happen—and I knew it with a novel and heady certainty.

I stood from the table and went upstairs to the bathroom, went upstairs to look at myself in the mirror. I wanted to see my face; I wanted for a moment to be alone with the truth of what I knew was coming. And when I came down the stairs again and stopped on the landing to see Chris's laughing face, to see the light around the table in a house that was otherwise entirely dark, I couldn't catch my breath. Not because I was afraid, but because I was—finally, fully, hopelessly—lit.

This was what I forgot that night, that warm night in late August when I began to fall in love with Chris: I was already in love. I had begun, in the months before the dinner party, to slip into the basement chapel of the Catholic Church down the street from my apartment, to kneel and stand and kneel again, to make the sign of the cross against what I had always thought to be a secular heart. I had fallen into belief, and into the consuming magic of the Catholic Church. I read the books of Thomas Merton on the subway; I worried a strand of rosary beads each morning before I left for work, reciting the prayers from an index card until I committed them to memory. I was both a stranger and my truest self in those days: I didn't fully understand how my life had taken this unexpected turn, and I also didn't know how I had not taken it sooner. I thought about God nearly all the time, although I did not speak about my belief to any of my friends. My silence—my absences, my lies of omission—separated me in a way that only I could see, and while at times I regretted the distance, I did not seek to close it.

Until that night. I lingered at the table; I let the last R5 train to Center City leave without me, knowing perfectly well that all the bedrooms in Jen's Main Line house were filled with sleeping children and out-of-town guests. And when Chris said—to Jen, not to me—"She can sleep at my apartment, if she wants to," I did not want anything but her.

It was nearly 2:00 a.m. when Chris and I left Jen's house and walked the three dark blocks to her apartment. She told me it was a relief to be back in Philly, that Jen was like a sister to her, and she had moved to the Main Line because she needed trees and quiet after her years in Manhattan. I didn't tell her I had moved downtown to escape the trees and the quiet. Instead I told her I knew her law firm, that it was a few blocks from my apartment.

"You'll have to excuse the mess," she said as I followed her up the stairs of her building, a stairway far brighter and grander than mine. "I was in Boston last weekend, my cousin's wedding. I was the maid of honor," she said, "if you can believe it." She spoke with an intoxicating mix of arrogance and intimacy, as though I knew her far better than I did. "I embarrassed my mother," she continued, "because the dress didn't cover my tattoo." We were in the hallway then, walking toward her door, and she stopped walking and turned toward me. "The straps went like this," she said as she leaned in to trace a long, slow line down my back with her finger.

Basement Chapels | 2

I saw Chris again the next weekend, when she took me to dinner
at the White Dog Café in West Philly, a restaurant I had
only ever been to with parents—mine and my ex-boyfriend's—
because no one I knew could pay the bill in a restaurant like that.
Chris and I sat at a corner table lit only by a small lamp with a
velvet-tasseled shade. All the food in the restaurant came from the
farms around Philadelphia, which was a novel concept in 1997. We
ate urban-garden lettuce topped with bright-yolked eggs and Lan-
caster County lamb chops. And we drank wine. I was twenty-three
years old and I could not remember being happier. After dinner
we went home together, and I stayed with her until late Sunday
evening when I rode the train back to my apartment, and on Monday morning I didn't take a shower because I did not want to wash
the smell of her from my body.

I didn't tell any of my friends about Chris. She was still too
private, too unexpected. They wouldn't disapprove, I was certain
of that, but still I didn't want to hear questions I had no answers
for. There was only one person I knew I would tell, despite the
fact that he was the one person who I knew would disapprove. It
was my therapist, and in those days I told him everything.

But not right away. I gave myself a week, and then two, and
then one more. Three weeks after that dinner at the White Dog
Café, and a month after I had first gone home with Chris, I finally

told him. "I met someone," I said. "A woman, actually." I tried to seem nonchalant on this point, although I failed. "I went home with her."

He looked at me for a moment. His face was expressionless. "You're not ready for a relationship," he said. "She's a distraction, and it won't last. But you know that already, don't you?"

My therapist's name was Hector, and he was nothing if not predictable. I had been seeing him for nearly a year by the time I met Chris, a year of Tuesday afternoons when I would knock on his door and a few seconds later he would open it, always dressed in a dark shirt and black pants. He had gray, curly hair and a short, gray beard, and he was not much taller than me. With a cool hello he stood back for me to enter, to walk past him and into his office, which was actually a small apartment. In the beginning I would steal glances of the spartan kitchen and the formal living room, but I quickly lost interest in both. Clearly Hector did not live in this apartment; there were no clues about him to uncover in those rooms. After a few weeks I just went straight into his office. The room was big enough for a red leather couch and two red leather chairs, an oriental rug, and a small polished mahogany desk, where he stood to answer phone calls during my sessions, something he did—always to my surprise—a handful of times during the years I knew him.

Hector would then sit down across from me, put his feet up on an ottoman, take a sip from his glass teacup, and wait for me to speak. At our first session I filled the air with backstory and anecdotes, all of which I believed to be highly insightful and revelatory. I paused near the end of the session, having run out of things to say. Hector put down his teacup, leaned back slightly in his chair, and said, "I don't have any idea who you are." He looked right at me and I looked back. I wanted to be insulted, but I could only be astounded that I had found my way to this person, this one person in all the world who could see me. To everyone else I was the confident young woman with the job she had been told she was too young for, the woman who got a phone call from the saleswoman at Saks when the dress she wanted went on sale, the woman who swam a fast mile every night after work. But in Hector's office those details did not a person make. According to Hector, my center—if I even had one—did not hold. I wasn't certain how he knew this, and that he did gave me a sense of anxious exhilaration.

I was steeped in unhappiness when I first came to Hector. I was in a failing relationship and didn't know how to end it. I had become a person so unrecognizable to myself that I avoided my eyes in the mirror; I cringed at the sound of my falsely cheerful voice on the outgoing message of the answering machine I shared with the boyfriend I was afraid to leave.

But after my first few sessions, Hector and I didn't talk about my boyfriend much. We talked about God. In the nearly twenty years since I met Hector I have tried to remember how our first theological discussion began, but I simply can't remember which one of us first mentioned God. I suppose I did; Hector didn't initiate conversation. What I do remember was how fragile I felt in his office after that first visit, how quickly it became clear that if I wanted to keep Hector's attention, if I wanted to please him, then I would have to dive deep and unearth some nugget of truth about myself that had nothing to do with my boyfriend, or my job. One thing I had begun to suspect about myself was that I was a believer, although I didn't know in what. But I did know that faith might be one true thing about me, and if that was what Hector was after, we could start there.

At one session, early in the time I knew him, I talked for a few minutes about work, about my friends, until—for the first time—Hector interrupted me. "Do you know the story of the virgins and their lamps?" he asked.

I was startled by his interruption. "No," I said.

"I don't remember it well, but it's something about ten women waiting for the midnight arrival of a man, and the man is really God. The women all have lamps, but only some of the women were wise enough to take oil for their lamps so when the man, the bridegroom I think he's called, arrives, the women with the oil can go in to him, but the others can't."

Hector paused and looked at me. I didn't say anything.

He continued. "The story is about doing the work. It's about being prepared, knowing what you'll need to get what you want. I think you want to know yourself, and I *think*," he said with emphasis, "that you want to know God." He reached over for his teacup. "You can't waste any more time with someone else's God, someone else's idea of a good life. You have got to stop looking for the shortcut."

Later, when I was no longer seeing Hector, I would wonder why it hadn't seemed strange for him to use a Bible story to elucidate his point. He was not, after all, a priest or a spiritual advisor. Hector was a therapist, and I knew almost nothing about him or what he believed. But that imbalance didn't concern me then. I had come to depend on his astute comprehension of me, and on his reliably undivided attention. And he was right: I did want to know God.

When young women like me were curious about God there were a few things we were expected to do: trek through India and Nepal; spend the winter washing dishes in a Benedictine monastery in Minnesota; volunteer at Mother Theresa's hospital in Nairobi; or, if we were really serious, enroll for a nondenominational Master's of Divinity at Harvard. But I wasn't doing any of these things. I was going to therapy on the eleventh floor of an upscale apartment building in downtown Philadelphia with a man whose own beliefs were a total mystery to me.

I have often wondered if Hector bellowed the fire of belief in all his young and drifting patients, if an entire cast of us came into his office so he could nudge us toward something larger than our-selves because our selves were too nascent, too nebulous to plumb with any success. But at the time this did not occur to me. At the time what Hector and I said to each other in that office had surely never been said before.

It's time to move out," Hector said on a February afternoon, six months after I had started seeing him. I had told him, yet again, that I wanted to leave my boyfriend. "Clearly you're not com-mitted, and it's time to move out. Forget about the lease and the rent, forget about the inconvenience. He'll manage. You're not a piece of furniture."

Hector's occasional but emphatic directives no longer startled me. In fact I had come to crave them. I wanted nothing more than for him to tell me what to do. That night I told my boyfriend I was moving out as soon as I could find an apartment, and the next morning I began my search.

By March I was living in a new apartment, far from the leafy resi-dential neighborhood where I had lived with my boyfriend, and a few blocks from Hector's office. "I'm so happy," I told Hector, "And there are so many things I want to do, you know? Things I didn't expect to want. I feel like going dancing. And last night I bought cigarettes and smoked in the bathtub."

Hector laughed. "Those sound like the things a child would do with this new freedom. But you aren't a child. And you didn't leave because you wanted a chance to do those things, did you?"

I looked away. "No," I said. "Of course not." This is what I didn't say: I'm twenty-three years old, Hector. That is exactly why I left.

Hector was impatient. I might have been young, but he wanted me to get moving. He suggested that I read Thomas Merton's spiritual autobiography, *The Seven Storey Mountain*. I bought the book and read it on the subway, on a stone bench in Rittenhouse Square, at my small kitchen table with a bowl of cereal holding the pages open. I finished the book on a warm Saturday afternoon and did not know what to do with the rest of the day or what to do at all, ever again. It was one thing to read about Merton's love for poetry and jazz and drinking, about his early and earnest search for God in basement chapels. His wit, his impulsivity, his narcissism—they were all enchanting and familiar. But the book's later chapters, which chronicled Merton's conversion, hurt my eyes with their brightness, their ardent cataloging of one renunciation after another, each one required—insisted upon—by God. On that Saturday afternoon in my Philadelphia apartment, I finished *The Seven Storey Mountain*, closed the book, and wedged it between two others on the shelf. I went to my dresser and picked up a few dangly earrings and a tube of lipstick. I opened my closet and flipped through the hanging dresses. You want all this, I told myself. I didn't mean the actual things, the clothes and the jewelry, the material possessions. I meant this world, this life. I was trying to remind myself, in the only way I could in that moment, that I was in the world and of it, which was exactly where I wanted to be.

"Why do you think you did that?" Hector asked me when I told him what I had done when I finished the book.

"Because I was afraid," I said.

"Of what?"

"Of what I wanted when I finished the book."

"Which was?"

"God," I said, surprised at how easy it was to say, and how there, in Hector's office, I was not frightened of anything at all.

At the end of the session I asked Hector what he thought I should read next. "How about the Bible?" he said. "You could start with the Gospels."

It seemed like a strange suggestion. Did people like me read the Bible? Couldn't I just read something *about* the Bible? I knew some standard verses from a few years of Sunday school at the Methodist church my parents joined when I was eight and they— two lapsed Catholics—decided it was time to get their children some religious education. But I couldn't recall a single story about Jesus—the very idea of him seemed rather embarrassing. It was the physicality of him, how ubiquitously and oddly he was depicted in American culture. The long hair, the flowing robes, the sandals. Jesus sandals. All over Philadelphia I saw images of him on billboards and buses, demanding repentance, loyalty, and the end of all abortions. He was human but strange. He was a caricature.

But despite all that, I read the Gospels, and they stunned me. They were nothing like I had imagined. The language had a hard and declarative edge that was as poetic as it was spare. Not a wasted word. After a few nights of reading I could hear Jesus's voice when he spoke. I liked his obtuse metaphors and his starkly beautiful language, something that I had assumed belonged only to the Psalms or the prophets. I loved the healing stories, especially the story in Mark about the blind man who, when asked by Jesus if he can now see, says, "I see men, but they look like trees, walking." Jesus touched the blind man's eyes again, and he is fully healed. Later, much later, I would think of that story. I would think that in those early days of faith I was like the blind man, only I had been touched just once and what I saw of God, what I knew of him, was a shadow, a trick of my eyes. Like trees, walking.

When I was too tired to read, I would lie in the darkness and think of Jesus. I was both excited and overwhelmed by the idea of him. How had I, in these few short months, moved from a general interest in spiritual matters to the uncool and oft-ridiculed world of Jesus lovers? Suddenly I didn't care how. I was there, and I was besotted. I began to read the great Catholic thinkers, the philosophers and poets and mystics, and in everything I read, Jesus seemed to fly off the page—he was a feeling, he was a voice, he was sweet relief from the loud world and my new loneliness in it. And then one spring night he was in my apartment.

I was sitting alone on the edge of my futon and suddenly Jesus was next to me, right there on the edge of my futon, and he was wearing the softest flannel shirt in the world. His hands were rough and his voice was warm and low, and for the moment he spent with me, he was extraordinarily good company. And in the moments that followed, when he had vanished and left me to wonder if he had been there at all, I looked at my hands, at the worn edges of my sheets, the stack of books on my bookshelf, and I wondered if being alone would always feel the way it did right now, if solitude would always feel this warm, this brimming.

The morning after Jesus came to me, I woke and went to work, as I did every weekday morning. I was working for an early education project in the Kensington neighborhood, which was poor and dense with the detritus of poverty—broken strollers and burned out cars by the curb, electric lines strung with sneakers. It had taken me a long time to get used to the sharpness of the place, the absence of shelter and shade. But I did, and I loved my job and the people I worked with, although I didn't live in their world. So I did my job that day. I cataloged Spanish children's books and helped a woman fill out her childcare license application, and then took the subway back to Penn Station and walked the six blocks to my apartment. All day I wondered if Jesus would come to me again. He didn't come that night, or the next, or ever again, at least not in the same way. But I continued to feel him near me, and I came to know him in a way that I knew nothing and no one else. What I believed he knew about me, and what I knew about him, had little to do with time or circumstance or language. Moments when I felt him with me were bent in time, so that even an instant contained my every embarrassment, my every mistake and excess of pride, and I sensed that I was entirely visible, and treasured. Being with him was like being in a room filled with mirrors, only without the impulse to look down or away. Let's just look, I could hear him say. Let's look and not be afraid.

In late spring, a few weeks after my visitation from Jesus of the Futon, and a few months before I would meet Chris and fall in love with a woman for the first time in my life, I walked past a Catholic church and decided to go in. Not into the church itself, but rather into its basement, where doors were propped open to a small and dark chapel, so dark that its stained glass windows remained black where they were meant to be sky blue, reddish yellow where they were meant to shine golden on the face of Christ. The walls were lined with chipped and fading statues, each one edged by several rows of candles in metal holders. People knelt in front of the statues and lit the candles with thin wooden sticks, then extinguished the sticks in a shallow tray of sand.

I knelt in front of a statue of Mary, her blue robe swirling at her feet, and I lit a wooden stick, and then a candle. A small woman with a scarf tied around her head knelt down next to me and gestured for my still-lit stick. I carefully handed it to her and as I did, as I knelt there in front of the statue, beneath the stained glass windows, surrounded by the smell of incense and the coolness of the stone floor and darkness of the pews, I was certain—absolutely certain—that I had found what I was looking for.

I returned to the basement chapel the next day, which was Saturday, for five o'clock Mass. The service was odd and campy and tinged with magic. Sit, kneel, stand, cross your forehead, cross your lips, cross your heart. Pass the peace. Call out to God, to the priest at the altar, to whoever was listening. I could barely follow. I loved it.

The next Tuesday I told Hector that I had gone to Mass. "I wanted to take communion so badly," I said. "I know there are rules, I know I wasn't supposed to, but I did. I couldn't help it."

Hector laughed. "I love your spirit," he said.

I was stunned. Was he supposed to say something like that? Was he supposed to love anything about me? But if I was stunned, I was also thrilled. Thrilled that I could be out on this unexpected and unexplainable edge of myself and be loved.

And now it was September, and I had been seeing Hector for a year; I had been attending Saturday afternoon Mass at the Catholic church—which I now knew as St. Patrick's—for several months. I was enamored with St. Patrick's by then, though I still didn't quite understand how, or even why, an uncertainty that had made me only more dependent on Hector—on our time together—to animate my new ideas, to explain my unexpected desires. My life didn't make sense without him. But now he was telling me I couldn't see Chris.

"Why don't you talk to the priest at St. Patrick's about it," Hector suggested. "Ask him if he thinks it's a good idea right now."

Even then I knew this was a manipulative suggestion. It wasn't a Unitarian church I had wandered into that Friday afternoon in spring. I was caught up in Catholicism, one of the most harshly and unapologetically homophobic denominations in the world. And while I was certain that Father Dowling would have no qualms about me being in a romantic relationship (he saw me as just another curious young woman, not the fledgling mystic Hector fancied me to be), both Hector and I knew he would disapprove of Chris simply because she was a woman. How much of Hector's enthusiasm for my Catholicism was now tangled up with his censure of my lesbian love affair? I was too afraid to ask. All I knew was that I didn't want to lose Catholicism or Chris, and I most certainly didn't want to lose Hector's approval.

"I'll talk to Father Dowling," I said, even though I had no intention of talking to Father Dowling.

I had waited until the end of our session to tell Hector about

Chris and now we were out of time, and so I gathered my things and said good-bye and told him I would see him again next week.

A few hours later Chris came to my apartment and I didn't mention anything about Hector, but in the morning I woke and immediately thought of him. I heard his voice in my head: she's a distraction. I got out of bed, took a shower, and when Chris and I were in the kitchen half-dressed for work and drinking coffee, I told her that this was happening much too fast, that my life was much too complicated for this to work, although I never actually said what "this" was, never actually explained why my life was too complicated for it.

"I like you so much," I said. "And I can't be with anyone, not now, so I think we should stop before . . ." I paused, not knowing what to say. "You know, before." I didn't finish the sentence.

"I understand," Chris said. She told me that a relationship wasn't what she wanted, either. I smiled, and nodded, and tried to appear confidently and maturely resigned, as though I slept with people and then stopped sleeping with people all the time.

We left the apartment together, went downstairs to the street to say good-bye. A few seconds later she turned and called back to me, "You know, I think it might already be too late." Then she waved to me with a swing of her briefcase and turned around again. For a moment I didn't know what she was talking about, and by the time I did she was gone.

3 | The Long Loneliness

In early October, a week after I broke up with Chris, I joined a class at St. Patrick's for people who wanted to be confirmed in the Catholic Church. I didn't know that I wanted to be confirmed, but I did want to be more than a visitor at Mass. I told Hector I was thinking of joining the class even though I wasn't really sure it was the right thing to do.

"Join," he said. "Keep moving and see what happens. You know," he continued, "eventually you won't need the Church. If you continue on this path, you will move beyond it. But for now, the Church is a good place to be."

I was intrigued by this idea of becoming some sort of post-Church visionary, but like so much of what Hector said I might someday be or have, the possibility belonged to an excruciatingly distant future. Still, I joined the class. It met at the rectory on Monday nights and was mostly composed of women who were engaged to devout Catholics. There was one young man in the class, a doctoral student in religion at Penn. He had taken the class twice already.

We met in the rectory's dining room around a gleaming wood table; the priest sat at the head. The class was intended to be an introduction to Church doctrine, which I suppose it was, albeit a unique one. Father Dowling was a deep thinker. He spoke in what sounded liked an epic religious poem, a rhythmic and repeating stream of words that he sustained for nearly the entire hour. By the time the class was over, his cheeks were flushed with exertion and my head hurt. Later I would look over my notes and see that they were nothing more than a list of words: *the distance of sin, broken world, seeking union.* Clearly I had missed something. Perhaps that is always the case when someone speaks to you in poems.

In reality I think I was only tuned to certain things Father Dowling had to say. In those days I wanted the fire; I was all about the rigor. When someone asked me if I had found comfort in the Church, I was taken aback. I wasn't looking for comfort. I wanted transcendence. I wanted Thomas Merton's astonishment. Later when I had moved away from Philadelphia I wrote to Father Dowling at Christmas and he wrote back, his tiny print covering one side of a St. Patrick's correspondence card. How glad he was to hear from me, he wrote, and he truly hoped that I was well and happy and loved. The card thrummed with affection and cheer. Had I received such a thing from him in those days in Philadelphia I would have been disappointed.

In the days when I knew Father Dowling I was seeking two different—and equally unobtainable—faiths. I wanted an ecstatic and consuming one, but I also wanted a softer one I could wear like an old coat. One that I had steeped in since birth, so that it was as inalienable as my own hands and inoculated against the prejudices and constraints of organized religion. The trouble with the first faith was that it was both too rigid and too vague; the trouble with the second was that it would have required a retroactive conversion, a divine grandfathering in. But I couldn't discern how untenable my desires were. So to serve the first possibility I read the Desert Fathers and *The Cloud of Unknowing* and taped lines from Hildegard of Bingen poems on my bathroom mirror. To serve the second I kept rosary beads on my nightstand and knotted palm fronds on my bookshelf. I never missed Mass, and when I was there I began to receive communion, despite the church law forbidding non-Catholics from receiving. But I didn't care. I wanted it. So I took my place in line, held out my hand for that tiny slip of wheat, and let it dissolve in my mouth. "The body of Christ," the priest would say to me before handing me the wafer. And even though I was certain about little in those days, I knew exactly what he was talking about.

I can see now that communion was why I decided to be confirmed with the rest of the class. I could have continued to receive without confirmation, but I wanted the Eucharist to be mine in all the ways it possibly could. And I wanted to keep meeting Jesus there in front of the altar. I hoped that soon the Jesus I was certain of and the God I was not would become—as I had been promised they were—one.

On a good day I was hopeful that such a time would come. But as fall ended and winter began, there were fewer and fewer good days. I couldn't stop thinking of the verse in Matthew that tells us not to store up treasures for ourselves on the earth: "For wherever your treasure is, there will be your heart too." This frightened me. My treasure was not my wardrobe or my filled bookshelves or my sixty-dollar haircuts. I loved those things, but they were not my treasure. My treasure was Chris. And it was becoming increasingly clear that breaking up with her hadn't made me love or want her any less, and it wasn't likely it ever would.

In mid-December I was, once again, in Jen's kitchen. I was nervous; I knew that Chris had also been invited to dinner and seeing her didn't seem like the best idea. Of course if I had been serious about keeping my distance I could have declined Jen's invitation. But I wanted nothing more than to see Chris. I thought of her every day.

At dinner Chris and I sat across the table, careful to avoid each other's gaze. Jen asked for news, and I announced my newly hatched plan to leave Philadelphia, at least for a little while. "I'm going to Colorado," I said. "Next fall. I'm planning to take a three-month sabbatical from work, although I might not come back." I looked at Chris, who was looking down at her plate.

When we had all finished eating, Jen and her husband stood to clear the dishes and the other guests went to the porch for a smoke. Suddenly Chris and I were alone. She looked directly at me for the first time all evening. "Come home with me," she said. And I did.

The next month was scattered with nights we spent together, awake until three, four, five in the morning. The clock had never spun so quickly in my life. In the morning one of us would leave and I would say, I can't do this, and Chris would say fine, but please don't call me, and I would say I wouldn't call. But then I would, and after a few cool minutes she would ask me where I wanted to meet.

I couldn't give her up. Before Chris my attraction to women had been ephemeral—a woman might thrill me just with the sound of her voice, or the way she rolled the sleeves of her shirt, but the way that I wanted her would have nothing to do with the ideas I held about the trajectory of my life, my future. Chris changed all that. One night soon after that December dinner party, I pressed myself against her in the hallway of her apartment and was startled by the solidity of her body, solid and smooth as planed wood. And the next morning when I sat with her on the train and watched as she scribbled notes on a legal pad, watched how every few minutes she would pull a torn-edged *New York Times* crossword out from behind the pad to fill in a few clues then slide it back again behind her work, I knew that there was nothing ephemeral about my desire for her. I knew that if I did not make the future I wanted happen—somehow—with her that I would never know such perfect solidness again, and I would wish for it always.

But the timing, the timing was terrible. This is what I told myself. Once or twice I brought up Chris in my therapy sessions—never actually telling Hector that I was still seeing her, that I was, in fact, still sleeping with her—and I would try to convince him that everything could be mine, that I could have Chris and still keep my tiny faith burning. That I could still be a Catholic. But the Church didn't believe that was possible, and neither did Hector. He didn't condemn my desires on religious grounds; he only claimed (at least overtly) that she was causing me to commit the sin of distraction. And it was true; Chris was a distraction. The most beautiful, exciting distraction that had ever crossed my line of vision. And try as I might, I could not turn away.

Now, all these years later, it occurs to me that I was conflating Hector and God, or that at the least I was taking Hector's word as definitive when really his word was just his own, when really he was only one man who pushed me too hard, the way a father might, the way my own father did not. It also occurs to me that I was an ideal therapeutic patient. I was diligent, engaged, and twenty-four years old. Who among us can resist the urge to tell a twenty-four-year-old what to do? Hector found in me a person who would, for a little while, do what he said. And I found in him a person who made the complexities of my psyche seem singular and intriguing, and, in many ways, beautiful. He must have known what he gave me, and he must have found it gratifying to offer. I can see that now. And I can see that he should have known better.

By February I was seeing Chris nearly every day. And I was still seeing Hector every Tuesday, but I no longer mentioned Chris at all. We talked only about God. Hector suggested I read *The Long Loneliness*, Dorothy Day's autobiography. I read it, jumping at the chance to do something to please him, to lessen my feelings of betrayal. The book terrified me. Day writes of her love affair with

Forster Batterham, who was, like Day before her conversion, a communist and an atheist. He would not marry Day on philosophical grounds. And so she separated from him, despite the fact that he was the father of her child, despite the grief it caused her. "Becoming Catholic would mean facing life alone," Day wrote, "and I clung to family life." But she released the domestic future of her dreams. And how right she had been to do it, for only then could she come to know God, only then could she discern his desires for her. Only then could she become the Dorothy Day who changed the world.

Years later Dorothy Day's letters were released for publication in a book titled *All the Way to Heaven*. I ordered the book from interlibrary loan and it arrived at my country library from the College of the Holy Cross in Worcester, Massachusetts. The book's first section contains nine years of letters between Dorothy Day and Forster Batterham. In *The Long Loneliness*, Day tells her readers that she separated from Batterham, once and for all, in December 1927. But her letters tell a different story. Day wrote to Batterham steadily until 1932, proclaiming her love and her desire, her wish for him to change his mind and agree to marry her. "Do write to me, dearest sweetest," Day wrote from California in 1929, "because I think of you and want you night and day." And in January 1932, after a night together: "What do you say you marry me . . . ?" This is what I had not fully understood when I read *The Long Loneliness*: Dorothy Day *adored* Forster Batterham. Even after she converted to Catholicism she wanted to marry him, but he would not marry her. Eventually she stopped asking. But in one of the last letters in the book, written two years before her death at eighty years old, Day told a friend that she spoke with Batterham nearly every day.

Would it have mattered if I had read Day's letters when I was twenty-four years old and trying to decide between God and Chris? Perhaps not. Perhaps then I would only have flipped ahead to torture myself with Day's final good-bye to Batterham. But I can say with certainty that the letters matter to me now. I read them and know that Day wanted a lover and she wanted God. And regardless of what Day was ultimately granted, our shared longing is enough for me.

Let a Joy Keep You 4

Spring came, and Chris and I were still together. A few days before Easter a package arrived from the Metropolitan Museum shop. I opened it to find another box, this one red and glossy and stamped with a swirling gold *M*. "Who's it from?" Chris asked. It was late; we were finishing take-out sushi at my kitchen table, and I had convinced her to sleep over even though she had an early meeting. I no longer sent Chris away every morning before dawn. And I no longer confessed anything to Hector. I kept my ambivalence from both of them, or at least I thought I did. I knew I couldn't keep it from them forever; I was just hoping to make it to the end of the summer. In September I was leaving for Colorado, and while I knew that I would, most likely, come back to Philadelphia, I fantasized that three months away would transform me into a person who knew exactly how to weave these tangled strands of desire and belief into an orderly, harmonious, and decidedly adult sort of life.

"I'm not sure," I said, although I had a pretty good idea. Inside the box was a gold cross hanging from a delicate chain and a small white card on which my mother had written a line from a Carl Sandburg poem: *Let a joy keep you. Reach out your hands and take it when it runs by.* I didn't read the card aloud.

"So this weekend I'm doing something kind of crazy," I said

to Chris before I lifted the cross from the box. "I'm becoming a Catholic."

Chris looked surprised, but she didn't say anything. Had I even mentioned the Catholic Church before now? I might have made a few offhanded comments about going to church, and I didn't move the Bible or stack of Thomas Merton journals from my bedside table on the nights that she slept over, but that was about the extent of my disclosure. Chris knew nothing about Jesus of the Futon; she knew nothing about Hector.

"It's sort of a last-minute decision," I said, realizing how ridiculous that sounded. I wanted to say something to her about how it didn't mean anything about us, or how I felt about her. I wanted to tell her that what I loved about Catholicism was on an entirely different plane from the hatred and prejudice of the institution. But Chris had been raised Catholic, she had suffered terribly because of that hatred, and I—in a blessed moment of common sense—knew enough not to suggest that such a division would be anything more to her than spin.

"Can I help you?" she asked, putting her hands out for the necklace I was struggling to clasp around my neck.

"I've got it," I said.

When I think about that night now, all these years later, I am struck by how patient Chris was, how careful. And how confused I must have seemed. Years later she would tease me, "Can you believe I didn't run?" No, I would say, in all seriousness. I can't.

I put on the necklace, went into the bathroom to look at it in the mirror. I had not worn a cross before. I pressed it against my bare neck and felt its pointed edges on my skin. I smiled into the mirror. The cross looked right; wearing it was the most effortless step I had taken toward God.

"So when exactly are you doing this?" Chris asked from the kitchen.

Let a Joy Keep You   27

"Saturday night," I said. "At the Easter Vigil service." I didn't ask her if she wanted to come; she didn't ask if she could.

The next morning Chris left early. I woke to the sound of her rummaging through her briefcase for a taxi voucher. She was dressed in her gym clothes, her faded Zen Palate T-shirt and running shorts. She looked over at me. "How about dinner?"

"It's Holy Thursday," I said, "so I'm going to church."

"And after?" she asked.

"You can take me to dinner," I said with a smile. In the last few months I had been in more restaurants that I had in the decade before I met her. And I had enjoyed every bite of food, every drop of wine. Sometimes Chris walked the few blocks from her law firm to my apartment after working late and instead of ordering food, I made her simple things, spaghetti with pesto, chicken salad, cookies that I baked in my toaster oven. She loved everything I fed her, loved that I wore boiled wool slippers in the kitchen and a short, black skirt instead of sweatpants. She loved the way I held my tongue between my front teeth when I danced in front of the stove, something I didn't even know I did. Until I met her it had not occurred to me that someone could find such pleasure in all the things I did without trying.

At my first Good Friday Mass I didn't want to venerate the cross. I didn't want to bend and kiss it, although I did want to be the sort of person who would. I wanted to be the sort of person who had venerated the cross every Good Friday of her life, who was propelled by ritual and habit, by her little-girl memories of watching her own mother bend toward a wooden Jesus. I had a Rumi poem taped to my bathroom mirror: *Out beyond ideas of wrong and right there is a field. I'll meet you there.* The field of my dreams was not beyond wrong and right so much as it was beyond deciding, beyond this bewilderment about exactly who I was hoping to become.

Let a Joy Keep You

I waited in the long procession to the front of the church, and I liked the waiting, I liked the slow shuffle of people in front of me, people behind. I liked approaching the bright altar. When I arrived at the front of the church I put my hand on the warm wood of Jesus's bare leg, then turned and walked away.

After the service I went back to my apartment and called my Nana, who was just home from her own Good Friday service. "I didn't venerate the cross," I confessed.

"Oh, I never do," Nana said. "Too many germs."

At dusk I once again walked the two blocks from my apartment to church. I was going to my first confession. Father Dowling, like most priests, no longer used a confessional so there was no dark screen, no anonymity. We sat across from each other at a small table. "This is my first confession," I said, and he nodded, signaling me to begin. I can't recall with any certainty what sort of sins I confessed to, perhaps my penchant for white lies, for exaggeration, for gossip? What I do remember is that after I confessed I said I needed to say something, and I needed to be certain he understood that what I was about to say was not a confession. Father Dowling nodded his understanding, and I told him I had a girlfriend.

He paused before speaking. "Do you think you can stop seeing her?"

"No," I said.

"Then do you think you can pray about her, pray for guidance?"

For a moment I didn't speak. I knew what sort of guidance he was talking about. But I still said yes, that I could pray about her.

Well what did you think he would say, I asked myself later. I shouldn't have expected more. Why did I tell him, then? Because I wanted him to know. He had been extraordinarily kind to me, and I had grown to love him, his ruddy face and silver hair, his homilies that were never dogmatic or political and always told us the same thing: you are not alone. And so I didn't want him to approach me at the altar on Saturday night believing that I was someone I was not. It was as though I believed telling him about Chris would melt the sharp-edged pieces of my life until they were one.

When I arrived at St. Patrick's for the Easter Vigil, I saw Hector waiting by the door. The sight of him shocked me. I had never, even once, seen him outside his eleventh-floor office. "This is for you," he told me and handed me a small package. I thanked him awkwardly and put the package in my bag. I went inside and he went down the steps of the church and into the street. I stood by the door for several moments, trying not the think of what it meant that Hector had been here, that there was, in my bag, a package from him.

As I stood there composing myself I watched the Easter fire burn in a cauldron near the entrance to the church. Two priests fed the fire with last Sunday's palm fronds; the fire's ashes would be saved to mark foreheads on next year's Ash Wednesday. There were small slips of paper on a table so that worshippers could write out prayers and toss them into the fire. Years before I had visited the Wailing Wall in Jerusalem and watched while people tucked folded pieces of paper between the stones. I had no prayers then, but I tore a page from my journal and scribbled down my grandparents' names, then folded the paper, kissed it, and pressed it into the wall. Now I wanted to put a prayer into the fire but I didn't have one. The God I knew then was not the God of simple gratitude, of protection. The God I knew was one of disapproval.

And so I walked past the fire and into the sanctuary toward the pews that were tied off with thick, crimson-colored ropes and I moved the rope aside, pulled down a kneeler, and rested for a moment in the privacy of a bowed head and folded hands. Kneeling brought me to a moment of grace, which it had done without fail every time I bent down on that narrow beam of wood, and I was reminded that this humble posture was a sort of home for me in this world. But was that—or anything that I loved, or felt devoted to—enough?

The sanctuary dimmed into darkness and the cantor began to sing the Exsultet, the Easter Proclamation, and her voice and the words were, quite literally, sublime, and they swept away my worry. But then it was time for me to go to the altar with all the other catechumens, and it returned. I could rise or not rise—who would care? Who would not forgive me for staying in my seat? But I rose and followed the others; I repeated the words Father Dowling lined out for me. I received the Eucharist and returned to my seat, wishing I felt something other than relief that the time for deciding was over.

When I was back in my apartment that night, I opened the present from Hector. It was a small book in a red leather binding, its title printed in gold on the narrow spine: *The Imitation of Christ*. I knew of the book (Dorothy Day read from it every day during the months of her conversion) but had never seen a copy. The pages were filled with simplistic drawings of a Jesus I did not recognize and prayers about suffering and sacrifice. I closed the book. I took off my suit, peeled off my stockings, and lay down on my bed, exhausted. What was worse, I asked myself, the terror of the book or the terror that I didn't want it?

Hector was not the only person who gave me a book when I became Catholic. On Easter Sunday, instead of going to church, I took the train to Chris's apartment. "I have something for you," she said when I arrived, and handed me a book: *Leaves of Grass*. She was a Whitman devotee; she had told me she couldn't believe how little of him I had read. I thanked her, although I didn't open the book. I put it in my bag and asked her if she wanted to walk to the park. On the way we passed a small Baptist church. The cross on the lawn, which was six, maybe seven, feet tall, was completely covered in azalea blossoms. At the park we spread out a blanket, and we sat together, watching the children on the climber, the tennis players, the running dogs. We weren't speaking, only sitting next to each other, our shoulders touching, and I could feel her affection, and knew she could feel mine. After a few minutes Chris took out the paper and a pen for the crossword. She folded her sweatshirt into a pillow and lay down on the blanket, holding the magazine at arm's length to shield her face from the sun. I opened my bag and took out *Leaves of Grass*. Her inscription to me was on the title page: *For E—All truths wait in all things, they neither hasten their own delivery, nor resist it.*

❧

In August, a year after my first date with Chris, I told Hector everything. I was in love with Chris; I would not stop seeing her. He told me I had to choose.

"Are you saying that you won't see me if I stay with her?" I asked.

"I'm saying that there's really nothing for us to do if you are in a relationship," he said.

I was stunned. Was he telling me that I couldn't come back? "And you would say the same thing to me if she were a man?" I asked.

Hector paused. "I don't know."

Now it was my turn to wait for him to speak.

"I've worked with homosexual couples," he said slowly, "and it seems to me that there is not the same potential for the development of a mature, adult relationship." He looked at me. "You can, you could, have more."

My stomach tightened; I had trouble finding a breath. Hadn't I known this was coming? Hadn't he been saying this, in whatever ways he could, all along? But this time was different. We were no longer talking about the singular demands of my faith, about the pull of Catholicism and its convenient condemnation of my desires. We were no longer speaking of what I could lose, at some undetermined time in the future, if I didn't make the right choice. Hector was offering his judgment, and with it, an ultimatum. I looked at Hector, at the rug, at Hector again. I pulled my bag onto my lap and still I could barely breathe. "I think I'll go now," I said in barely a whisper.

Hector nodded. He did not look away as I rose from my seat, but he also did not follow me to the door.

I took the long way home from Hector's office that evening. I didn't want to be alone in my apartment; I didn't want to call Chris, or to see her. I was too humiliated to explain what had happened to me. How could I justify the extent of my trust in Hector, or the strange fusion of therapeutic and spiritual concerns that I shared with him? Who talks about God with their therapist? Or more to the point, who stays with a therapist who talks about God the way Hector does? I burned with shame. I felt, as I had so often in my life, like the worst sort of eccentric: not adventurous or inspired, but odd, out of step.

The next morning I called the friend who had referred me to Hector. I packed while we talked: I was moving to Colorado, where I planned to spend the next three months writing in my parents' empty house (they were on a cross-country bicycle trip) and traveling the Southwest. I no longer worked for the Kensington community organization, and the downtown nonprofit that I now worked for was willing to pay my health insurance while I was gone and give me a raise and a promotion when I returned—money that would pay for my months of not working. I would sublet my apartment, put my possessions in storage, and be free. This plan had seemed inspired a few weeks ago and now seemed exhaustingly impossible to execute.

"My god," my friend said when I finished telling her about my last session with Hector. "You know, he can't say those things to you."

"I know, I know," I said, although I didn't really know at all.

"Therapists have a lot of power, and it can be extremely difficult for a patient to discern when the advice isn't good. He's really, really homophobic."

I knew that Hector was homophobic, and I knew his views on same-sex relationships were wrong. This was one point on which he could not sway me. But the trouble was I couldn't see that this profound rift was an irreconcilable difference of belief, that the psychosocial legitimacy of same-sex relationships was not something on which we could agree to disagree. I couldn't admit that Hector had wronged me, terribly, by saying those things, and there was no going back.

"He is," I said, "but there's so much more to my relationship with him."

"Not now there's not," she said. "This changes everything."

After my friend and I hung up, I walked to a diner around the block for a good-bye lunch with my uncle, who was also a psychologist. When our food arrived I asked him if he had ever told a patient that he wouldn't see her if she didn't end a relationship. He thought for a moment before speaking. "Well," he said, putting down his sandwich, "I've had patients who were having affairs tell me they wanted to work on their marriages without ending their affairs." He smiled and rolled his eyes good-naturedly. "So then I've had to say, 'Well, then I really can't help you.'"

I heard Hector's voice inside my head say that's exactly what you are doing, metaphorically speaking. For how much longer, I wondered, would I hear Hector's voice inside my head?

I told my uncle about Chris and about Hector, about what he had said to me. When I began to cry my uncle reached across the table for my hand and smiled at me in the way he had been smiling at me since I was a young girl, a smile of affection and reassurance, a smile that I had known long enough to know that soon he would be laughing. "Oh, Hector Cruz," he said with an air of exaggerated, satirical prestige. He shook his head and laughed then, and I did too. It was the first time I laughed about Hector, and I would not laugh about him again for more than a decade.

After lunch I went back to my apartment to finish packing. The phone rang as I walked in the door. It was my uncle. "You know," he said, "therapists are wrong sometimes. What Hector did, what he said, was wrong."

Later that afternoon I saw Chris and told her what had happened. She thought it was absurd, that Hector was unconscionable, unprofessional, fucked-up. Her dismissal, unlike my uncle's, was no solace. It was, in fact, the opposite. We rarely spoke of him again.

I called Hector the first day I was in Colorado. He didn't pick up the phone, and I didn't leave a message. I didn't call him again.

Ordinary Beds | 5

I think we should go to Paris."

Chris and I were lying in bed on the morning of my twenty-fifth birthday. I had just finished opening presents from her: a Mont Blanc pen, an annotated edition of *Walden*, and a pair of small gold earrings. We were in Colorado and I was barely a month into my ill-conceived travel and writing sabbatical. So far I had spent most of my days crying and hiking on trails no more than ten miles from my parents' house. Before I left Philadelphia I told Chris that I wanted this time to be a break, and she said sure, we'll take a break. But she flew to Colorado almost every weekend. When she came we walked downtown together and browsed bookstores and ate Mexican food. We went to the movies and napped in the sun. And now she wanted to take me to Paris.

"Oh, I don't know," I said.

"Well, I'm going," she said. "I'm going for New Year's, and I would love for you to come with me."

"I'll think about it," I told her. But I didn't really need to think about it. I knew that I would go to Paris with Chris that winter. I had made my choice; I had chosen her. And while I still had no idea if it was the right choice, I didn't regret it.

Chris and I landed in Paris at dawn and went straight to the hotel. "My god, I'm exhausted," Chris said as she walked into the hotel room. She dropped her bag and started to undress. She pulled the duvet back from the bed. "Let's sleep."

"We can't sleep," I said. "We have to get ourselves on Paris time." I walked over to the double windows, which I realized were actually the doors to a small balcony from which I could see the Tuileries and its Ferris wheel, unlit and still. I turned back to look at Chris, who was now in bed, and at the room, which was green and gold and smelled like wealth. It smelled like nowhere I had ever been before. "We should walk," I insisted. "Or eat some breakfast."

Chris beat the pillow to fluff it, then flipped it over and lay her head down. She lifted the covers in invitation. "We're here for a week," she said. "There's no harm in a nap."

Chris did everything her own way, which was the most exciting thing about her. I crawled into bed with her that morning, and we slept until afternoon. We went out into the falling dusk and stopped at a café for omelets and wine, and when we had finished, the time on the clock no longer mattered. We weren't tired and there was plenty to do. And when we did tire, we pulled the heavy silk drapes over the balcony doors and slept. It was winter, and so the sun rose late and set in the midafternoon, and for the brief time it was in the sky it barely shone. Paris in December was cold and damp and gray. It was the most beautiful place in the world.

And it was so far from home. In Paris, Chris did not hesitate when I reached for her hand, did not pull back when I leaned across the café table to kiss her. And when, late one night we stood kissing against a building near the hotel and someone honked and called out a car window at us, she pulled away only to laugh. This was not the Chris I knew. A few weeks before, when we were still in Philly, we had run into a managing partner of Chris's law firm at a small neighborhood restaurant. "There's Henry," Chris whispered, straightening in her chair. When he came over to say hello, Chris introduced me as her friend. Henry insisted we join him and his son, which we did. And when dinner was over, Chris and I rose from the table, put on our jackets, and walked out the door. That dinner was the longest she had ever gone without touching me.

I, on the other hand, told everyone at my office about Chris. When she called me at work (this was before cell phones, before texting), she had a terrible of habit saying, "Erin White, please," when the receptionist answered the phone, as though I worked at the next law firm over instead of a community education project. "That was my girlfriend," I told the secretary the first time Chris called. "Sorry about her greeting." And then, by way of explaining, I told her that Chris was a commercial litigator, which was, in my world, more scandalous than her gender.

In truth, I preferred Chris's caution. In Philly, when we said good-bye without touching on the crowded train platform, we were the only two people in all the world who could imagine how our morning had begun. Our sex was a deep and arousing secret, a secret that had eased my inhibitions and cleaved me to her far sooner, far more deeply than I had been joined to anyone else.

When I think of my penchant for secrecy—as though it were a preference, a chosen pleasure—I am discomfited by how little I understood of what was really at stake. Chris had a job that, for many reasons, could not be jeopardized, one of the reasons being she had a family who had not entirely accepted her gayness. She was on her own, and had been for a long time. She hadn't lived at home since she was eighteen. She put herself through law school and when, at twenty-five, she graduated, she moved to New York City and began working the fifteen-hour days she was still working when I met her. She was always afraid of losing her job, despite the fact that she was a star.

Later, much later, when it would become essential for us not to keep secrets, for us to be clear about who we were to each other at all times for the sake of our children, I would see how our honesty lightened every last bit of Chris. How it would change her life.

During those days in Paris, Chris and I didn't want to see or do many of the same things. At the Louvre I wanted to see *The Lacemaker*; she wanted to see *The Coronation of Napoleon*. She wanted to find an Alsatian restaurant she had read about in a Hemingway novel; I wanted to find a crepe stand I had read about in a travel magazine. She wanted to read the plaque at the Place Vendôme; I wanted to walk the labyrinth at Chartes Cathedral. But even if we could not understand each other's desires, we were enchanted by them, because we were enchanted by each other. Chris walked miles through the Louvre to find that tiny Vermeer of my dreams; I ate blood sausage and sauerkraut for lunch and sat on a bench reading a novel while Chris deciphered Napoleon's worn invocation. And on a rainy afternoon that Chris surely would have rather spent in a dark bar drinking Cognac and daring me to smoke one more Gauloise Blonde, we took the high-speed train out of Paris to Chartres.

When we got to Chartres we found the labyrinth covered by row after row of chairs so that you could see its faded outline on the stone floor, but you could not walk the circling maze to the four-petaled bloom at its center. I was disappointed. I had secretly hoped that going to Chartres and walking the labyrinth would prove I could have this wild and improbable life, prove that I could rise from a hotel bed, naked and flushed from sex like I had never known with a woman—a woman!—whom I loved as I had loved no one else, and then, a few hours later, walk toward God on a meandering but certain path in one of the oldest Catholic churches in the world. I wanted to stand at the center of that maze and believe in every pleasure, every beauty, every possible union. But now it seemed that Chartes would not grant me this wish; now it seemed absurd that I had even hoped such a thing would be possible.

"Let's stay anyway," I said to Chris.

"Sure," she said. "Let's go in."

I wanted to be alone, and so when Chris stopped to look at the paintings in the first alcove, I kept moving into the cathedral, further and further from the light of its enormous doors, its rose window. I spent the afternoon in the cathedral close, walking from one nave, one chapel to the next. As I moved further I was surrounded by what appeared to me as artifacts of seeking, stone and glass and plated gold, all of it arranged to bid miracles. And they buoyed me. As I studied the statues of the saints, their stone faces impossibly expressive, I thought of the men who made them, their rough hands and patience, their tempers and mistakes. Did they pare these saints for love of God or money? For love of God, I decided. And this was the solace of Chartres: that once ordinary men rose from ordinary beds to cut glass and stone into the shape of devotion. Ordinary men who then turned back to the world, happy to see beloved faces around the table, happy to stretch their legs on gray stone streets.

"Are you ready?" Chris asked when I approached her in the narthex, where she had been waiting for me.

I nodded. "Let's go back," I said with a smile whose meaning Chris, by now, understood perfectly.

When I returned home from Paris, I told my parents about Chris. They were cautious and kind. My mother asked me if I thought this was a one-time affair, or more of a shift in identity. She was asking me if I was a lesbian now. I told her I hadn't really thought about it that way, by which I meant I hadn't thought of how to classify or explain myself, or how she might explain me to her friends and our family.

I hadn't thought about my relationship with Chris this way because I didn't want to. I wasn't interested in a new identity. I didn't want to be anyone but the girl I had always been, certain of her place in the world and in the culture, which is to say certain of her privilege, her wide range of access. I was blind to the reality that this wasn't a decision I could make, that no outsider, no matter her race, her money, or her education, could remain inside a culture that didn't see her as fully human. It would take me years to understand that I sought an impossible and shifting stance: I wanted to move between insider and outsider—straight and gay—as it suited, as I wished.

I wanted everything: to love a woman yet avail myself of the opportunities and status of straight culture; to break the rules of the Church but still feel myself beloved by it. My mother had asked me a simple question. And while I didn't know it at the time, a decade would pass before I could answer it with any honesty at all.

Wake | 6

"How are you going to introduce me?" I asked Chris.

We were sitting in the car outside a funeral home in Worcester, Massachusetts. Chris's grandmother's wake was going on inside. There were so many cars turning into the parking lot that a police officer was directing traffic. Chris had waved to the officer when she pulled in. "That's Robbie Donahue," she said, and then added, "My father directed funeral traffic to pay for Catholic school." Chris's father was a vice cop. Before graduating from the police academy at twenty-five, he was a helicopter mechanic and door gunner in Vietnam. Chris was born while he was at basic training; she learned to walk and talk while he was in Vietnam. According to family legend, Chris's younger sister was conceived in the taxi their parents took home from the airport the night he returned for good. Her father was near sixty now, and nowhere close to retiring. For years he had refused one promotion after another. Why, he asked, would he want to spend his life behind a desk? "I like the chase," he said.

"How should I introduce you?" Chris asked. She wasn't looking at me. I knew she didn't really want to deal with this. Not today.

"Just use my name," I said. "And leave it at that." I was putting on lipstick in the car mirror. Yesterday I had gone to Eileen Fisher, the only clothing store in the Massachusetts college town where we now lived, and tried to find something appropriate for a wake. I had been to only one wake before this, my own grandfather's, but that had been in Pittsburgh in March, at a time when I still had a real job and lived in a real city, and so I wore a brown suit and brown pumps and kept an extra pair of stockings in my purse in case I got a run. Now it was late June in Worcester, and I was a graduate student. I was wearing a black pencil skirt with a lime-green, sleeveless sweater, which was, I realized as I watched all the women walking into the funeral home in pale suits, a terrible choice. My hair was expanding in the humidity and I was starting to sweat.

"Why don't you go in first," I said. I didn't want to pressure Chris, not now. She missed her grandmother terribly. For the past three months she had spent every Saturday in Worcester with her grandmother, watching Red Sox games, doing crossword puzzles, eating the Ritz crackers and sliced cucumbers of her childhood. On those Saturday mornings Chris would get dressed early, fill her coffee cup for the car, and pack her bag for the day I had hoped we would spend together, now that we had made a home for ourselves in an old parsonage on the Main Street of a tiny Massachusetts town. On those Saturdays Chris would come home late, her eyes red from crying in the car. That spring I learned Chris was not as estranged from her family as she had once suggested.

Eventually I got out of the car and went into the funeral home. The reception room was filled with people and the thrum of conversation. I saw the casket, saw the long line of people waiting to kneel, make a rapid-fire sign of the cross, and then lay their hand for an instant on the glossy wood. I did not make an approach.

Instead I gave my condolences to Chris's parents, whom I had met once before, and they accepted them kindly but were quickly distracted. The line of people needing to speak to them was long. I was only relieved. I didn't have much to say to them. After a few minutes, Chris's sister Lynne found me in the lobby. "Tennis, anyone?" she asked with a laugh, nodding to the sweater I had tied over my shoulders in an attempt to dim the lime green without adding to the sweating problem. I had known Lynne for a few years by now. She was a wise-cracking and lively person, and I liked her. And while I was certain she had no problem with the idea of me, I couldn't tell if she liked the actual me.

Lynne opened her arms and gave me a hug. She always smelled the way I had, as a child, assumed I would smell someday, a floriated mix of perfume and makeup and hair product that did not overwhelm but still left no room for other, more animal smells.

"I'm so sorry about your nana," I said.

"Thank you," Lynne said. "I can't believe she's gone!" This is what everyone in the family had said when I offered my condolences. Their nana was eighty-five and had been in a state of decline for years. Still, it seemed no one could imagine life without her.

"Oh, and congratulations too," I said, looking down at her stomach.

"I heard the heartbeat today," Lynne said, giving her belly a pat, as though to praise what swam in there. "So I'm telling everyone." She laughed, swung her hand toward the crowd, and flipped her long, blonde hair over her shoulder. Lynne was a second-grade teacher at a local parish school, and she lived a block from the house where she was born. These were her people, and it was clear—and enviable, to me—that she would spend the wake offering the seed of hope that was her growing baby; she would walk among everyone as an antidote to death. It's not often these things line up this way, that you are the one bearing a new soul as an old one rushes out. I could see that she felt a lesser loss because of it, that she felt a bit invincible.

Lynne left me to continue on her rounds, and I sat down in the row of plush chairs against the wall to watch the action around me. Everyone was talking loudly; everyone, it seemed, had a pressing story to tell. The women had well-styled hair and wore lots of gold jewelry and bracelets that chimed when they moved their arms. They spoke with their heads close, their hands over their mouths. The men were clean-shaven and handsome in their suits, and they charmed me with their firm handshakes, their smiles, the way they crossed their arms over their chests and leaned in as they laughed. My own parents' friends were scientists and academics, social workers and textile artists. The men were wiry and mostly bearded, the women wore linen skirts and expensive scarves and let their hair go gray and wore it cut close to their heads. They tended toward thoughtful introversion. They were marvelous people, they were *my* people, but now, sitting here in O'Connor Brother's funeral home, I wanted to be one of these people too, to claim their exuberance, their shine, and, more than anything, their belief.

I also watched Chris, watched how she was laughing, listening intently to people's long answers to her questions, gasping with excitement at the sight of old friends and their babies. I had never seen her so enthusiastic, and I couldn't tell if it was an act. Later, after many years together, I would come to understand that it was not an act, that she adored these people, cherished her past with them. But I would also come to understand that when the retirement or first communion or graduation party was over and the time came for us to go home, she would need to sleep for hours, sit in silence at the table with the newspaper, or go for a run with her iPod blasting so that she could return to the world where she lived without them, the only world in which she could truly be herself.

That evening after the wake we went to Chris's parents' house. "Where are we sleeping?" I asked Chris. The last time Chris and I had spent the night at her parents' house (which had also been the first time), her mother put us in separate bedrooms. It seemed odd to me that she would still enforce their house rule of no shared beds until marriage despite our being already in significant violation of their more essential rules, but I didn't protest. And neither did Chris. She had shared a bed with high school girlfriends, but only because her parents had no idea what they were doing or who they were to each other. And after high school she didn't bring many girlfriends home with her.

"My mom said to share a room," she said. "There's not enough space to split us up."

"Lucky us," I said in a not particularly nice tone. Chris didn't say anything. After this visit her mother wouldn't try to separate us again, and I would begin to understand that this is how I would become part of the family, crossing one unmarked and unspoken boundary at a time.

In the morning, Chris and her cousins went to the church to prepare for the funeral, and I stayed behind. Her cousin Terri was going to read from Corinthians during the service; Lynne and Jen, Chris's youngest sister, who was twenty-five years old and still referred to as "the baby," would carry the wine and wafers to the altar for communion. Chris and her older cousins were pallbearers, she the only woman among them. No one, not even Chris's parents, mentioned anything about this distinction. No one seemed to notice. When Chris was eight years old, she was the first girl in all of Worcester to play Ty Cobb little league. This was five years before Title IX, and the story ran in national newspapers. Her strength and physical ambition were a source of confusion and discomfort to her parents; her father was an extraordinary athlete, and in all fairness so was her mother, although she never played team sports. But her father had been a baseball star, a natural. And he had no son. But he had Chris, who was also a natural, and he struggled to make his peace with his unconventional daughter. Her mother discouraged her from playing sports. She punished Chris when she spit through her teeth; she implored her to do the things the other girls liked to do. Chris told me this made her more determined to play, and to excel. I suspected that it also made her sad, and lonely.

Many years later, when our own daughters were old enough to play team sports, Chris's mother gave us a scrapbook into which she had pasted every clipping, every team photo, every sports section listing of Chris's remarkable stats. She had underlined Chris's name whenever it appeared, put a star next to her quotes. In one team photo, a blurry shot taken from some distance, she had drawn a heart around Chris's face.

When I arrived at Our Lady of the Angels, I went in through the side door then took a wrong turn, so instead of entering the sanctuary I went into the priests' quarters. Nine priests were serving at this funeral mass, in homage to Chris's grandmother, who had devoted herself to the Church. All nine of them were dressing, throwing white robes over their dark suits so that the robes caught the air for a moment, and the priests appeared as birds whose wings were puffed against a cold rain. I turned away before they saw me, or at least I hoped it was before. What I had seen seemed a secret, the way they had gone from being men to something else entirely.

I didn't sit with Chris at the funeral. I found a seat near the back with her cousin's wife, who was trying valiantly to keep her toddler quiet. A few minutes after the processional, the little girl started making too much noise and they left the sanctuary for the crying room, and left me alone in the pew. When the Mass ended, Chris and the other pallbearers walked out of the church with the coffin. I could see that Chris was weeping, and because she was carrying the coffin she could not wipe the tears from her face so they were falling onto the lapels of her suit jacket. I began to cry, because it was so sad to see her that way, and because she was not mine just then. She was her Nana's. And Chris could not belong to both of us, not in this life. She had told her Nana nothing of her gayness. And I knew that, consciously or not, Chris was allowing me to enter her family only as her grandmother was leaving because she didn't know if she could have us both, and she was scared to try.

After the funeral, Chris's parents' house swelled with people, and I tried to keep busy (and out of the way) in the kitchen. I sat for a little while with Chris's grandfather, who seemed to have aged a decade since yesterday's wake, and I chatted with him about baseball and the weather, two things I knew little about. He talked slowly, his eyes downcast. He didn't ask me who I was.

By four o'clock most of the guests had gone home. The mothers and aunts were in the kitchen drinking wine; the fathers and uncles were in the garage inspecting Chris's father's drag racing car. The grandchildren were in the basement, playing restaurant at the wet bar and goofing around on exercise equipment. We—Chris and I, her sisters and her cousins—were in the living room. Chris's sisters and cousins were adamant about their love and acceptance of Chris and had known many of her old girlfriends. But still I had the sense that they were a little uncertain about me. Chris had not brought many girlfriends home, and now here I was, not only in their house but at their grandmother's funeral, lazing around on the couch with them after all the other guests were long gone and only family remained.

After we had finished a few bottles of wine, Lynne started rummaging in her parents' entertainment center for old home movies. "Oh, let's watch this one!" she said, pushing a VHS tape into the player, shushing everyone by waving the remote control at us. In an instant the snowy screen became a vision of their nana in a pink sweatshirt, standing over the stove and talking to the camera about whatever it was she was making. Everyone in the room got quiet. "She's making blinis," Lynne said to me, then turned back to the screen.

"Like for caviar?" I asked. No one answered me; they were too busy watching, and crying, and laughing. They were, with the exception of Lynne, a little drunk.

"Oh, let's do it now," Chris's cousin Terri cried, tears running down her cheeks. "Let's make blinis!"

And then they were all saying, yes, yes, let's make blinis! Terri called into the kitchen, "Auntie Judi! We're making blinis!"

Chris's mother called back, "Not in my kitchen you're not!"

It was then decided, with murmurs and laughter, that in the morning, after Chris's mother left for her seven-to-three shift at the hospital where she worked as a cardiology LPN, we would make blinis.

"Wait until you taste them, hon," Chris said, putting her arm around me for the first time all day. "Just wait."

From what I could discern from the video, blinis were potato pancakes with a little extra flour. I was slightly awed by the fact that these people seemed to believe there was something distinctly Lithuanian about shredded potatoes fried in oil.

"Aren't blinis just latkes?" I said.

"No," Chris said, shaking her head. "They're different."

The next morning blini-making began right after breakfast. Lynne arrived with her little boy and her husband, Jim, a large and genial red-haired Scot. Jim was the son of a butcher, and a fantastic cook. The next year he would talk me through a standing rib roast over the phone, rescuing my near-botched Christmas dinner for the in-laws we would soon share. On this morning he had an electric skillet under one arm and a bag of potatoes under the other.

They all got to work washing and peeling, admonishing each other for deviating from Nana's technique, crying and laughing over their growing piles of potato peels. I offered to grate. "Okay," Lynne said, "but be careful. No fingernails in the blinis." I looked at Chris, wanting to share a horrified glance, but she had her back to me at the sink, scrubbing potatoes. "I think I can manage," I said.

Soon the skillets were warm, and Jim dropped alarmingly generous spoonfuls of Crisco into them. The snowy mounds began to melt into clear and smoking lakes of oil. Lynne squeezed the starchy liquid from the potatoes with her hands, then mixed them with egg and flour and dropped the mixture into the oil. Soon the house smelled like a McDonald's.

The smell brought in the uncles and aunts—who had been keeping their distance on the patio—for a plate of their child-hoods, fed to them by their grown children. And the kids came in from the yard, calling, I smell blinis! I was the plate filler then, putting two and three blinis on each paper plate, spooning apple-sauce for the children, sour cream for the adults, fielding requests for more. Chris and her cousins ate them without plates, standing up, with their fingers. For the first time since we arrived, everyone was quiet.

When it seemed that everyone was sated, I filled the sink with water and soap. Chris's mother would be home from work in a few hours, and the kitchen was a mess of dishes and potato peels. Jim came over and, wordlessly, took over the rinsing.

"Well," Lynne asked me. "How were your first blinis?"

"Oh, I loved them!" I said, hoping I was enthusiastic enough.

Jim turned and looked at me. He winked. "Give it time," he whispered. "Give it time."

Chris was twenty-five years old when she came out to her parents. It didn't go well. They were a working-class Catholic family, first-generation Americans, who still lived in the house they had moved into on their wedding day in the town where they were born. In our house we have a picture of Chris's mother, six years old, on Santa's lap. Chris's sister has a picture of their father, also six years old, with the same Santa. Their world was small, and while this fact alone doesn't explain their struggle to accept Chris's gayness, it did make them—would make any of us—more susceptible to the gaze of others, to the watchful eye of authority and its insistence that we do not get to do what we want just because it feels good. And it made it difficult to know when exactly—how exactly—you became an adult, became the one who gets to make the rules. To change them. Made it difficult for them to see the possibility of reinvention, of a life off script.

So when Chris came out, her parents were angry, and they were frightened, and they said hurtful things. She forgave them, bit by bit. By the time Chris and I met she had reached a fragile peace with them, a peace that was in large part dependent on Chris's discretion, and her undivided attention when they asked for it. She kept her romantic life private and her loyalty to them clear. She kept the peace. What I don't think any of them realized was that Chris had done it for her grandparents' sake. It was their approval she could not bear to lose, their affection she could not live without.

Chris's grandfather died three months after her grandmother. He wasn't sick, or even taking any medications when he died. He was tired, and he missed his wife too much. Chris and I sat together at his funeral, and after the service she introduced me to people as her girlfriend. At the luncheon following the service, I sat next to a priest wearing a large onyx ring and a cashmere blazer who told me stories of his years at the Vatican. Chris's grandmother's favorite priest was absent from the lunch. When Chris asked her father about him, he told her that last month there had been accusations of sexual abuse, a harrowing number of boys over a harrowing number of years. Now he was gone. To jail? Chris asked. Her father wasn't sure where he was. Well, thank God Nana didn't know, Chris said. It would have destroyed her. Chris's father nodded in agreement. Yes, thank God she died when she did. That she was spared the heartache. As I listened I couldn't help but think of the heartache Nana's death had spared me, and how secretly grateful I was to both Chris's grandparents for going when they did, and for giving me the chance to stay.

7 | Rules of Engagement

I proposed to Chris on a Saturday morning, just a few weeks after her nana's funeral. "I think we should get married," I said. "I think we should have a wedding." I was lying on the bed in our guest room and she was vacuuming ladybugs from the walls. I had been grading papers until she interrupted me with her daily ritual of ladybug extermination. Our house was infested with ladybugs; they seemed to hatch on particularly sunny days and congregate in the guest room. At first I liked them, and tried to convince Chris they were a sign of good luck. But soon enough they were in the shower and in the sheets and I came to accept the necessity of the vacuuming.

Chris turned off the vacuum. "Are you proposing?" she asked.

"I am," I said, "but you can still feel free to get me a ring."

Chris and I had talked about getting married long before I proposed. There would be no legal significance to the wedding; this was 2001 and federally recognized same-sex marriage was still fifteen years away. At the time we couldn't have imagined the speed with which states would begin to legalize gay marriage (our state being the first, no less), or that the Supreme Court would rule on the matter in just fifteen years. We couldn't have imagined that one day we would buy a new stove and name it after Edith Windsor, whom we had to thank for the federal tax return we bought it with.

But all that was still to come. It was 2001 and people still rallied for civil unions, still planned commitment ceremonies. I hated the idea of both. They were accommodations; to have either would suggest that the state—and the Church—could tell me what sort of life I was allowed to have. I wanted a wedding; I wanted to be married.

Looking back I admire my orthodoxy, delusional as it was. Delusional because whether I liked it or not, the state *could* tell me what sort of life I was allowed to have. Marrying Chris—and not a man—meant losing a whole host of rights and safeties. I was engaged in some serious magical thinking then, having decided I would marry Chris but still hold tight to my straight privilege. I might be marrying a woman, I silently announced to the world, but I'm the same as I ever was. I'm the same as all of you.

This delusion was made possible by a range of circumstances: I had lived as a straight person my whole life, and still easily passed. I looked like an Irish girl-next-door: long brown hair, manicured hands, lipsticked lips. My closet was filled with dresses and heels, my drawers with lace underwear and nightgowns. My only significant personal experience of homophobia—Hector—was one I had not yet reckoned with. And perhaps most essentially, we lived in western Massachusetts, a place where lesbians had so fully permeated the culture that even the sixty-year-old farmer who came to deliver our firewood didn't flinch at the sight of two women's names on the check. For these reasons, my delusion went on for longer—much longer—than it should have.

Chris, on the other hand, having known that she was gay from the time she was a young girl, knew exactly how the world saw her. She was okay with civil unions and had no interest in a church wedding. But she was still deeply pleased by the idea of our wedding, despite her constant insistence that she did not see herself as a bride. "You don't have to," I said every time she said it. And I meant it. I certainly saw myself as a bride and was happy to have the role to myself.

Chris got me a ring. It was an art deco sapphire, and we bought it together in an estate jewelry store in Provincetown a few weeks after my proposal. By then I was already planning our wedding, trying to decide when and where we might have it, who we would invite. I found a book about lesbian weddings, a guide to creating meaningful rituals. The book had poorly reproduced black-and-white photos along with narratives about a dozen or so ceremonies. Many of the rituals were pagan; several included creative ways of involving pets and former lovers. The book made Chris laugh, but it made me crazy. All these years later I can see that the book is a treasure, a marvelous document of revolution and bravery. I can feel a tenderness and camaraderie with those marrying women. But in the months before my own wedding they frightened me. They were so far afield, so removed from straight culture. I couldn't see myself or even my desires in those pictures. So I put away the book and instead studied *Martha Stewart Weddings*. I ripped pictures of flower arrangements from magazines, compared tent-rental prices, and weighed the relative merits of fig and nasturtium salad garnishes.

I also tried to get as much God into the ceremony as Chris would allow.

"What would you think about being married by a minister?" I asked Chris near the end of the summer. And then, before she could answer, I added, "If we can find the right one."

"It's fine," she said. "But not in a church."

"Oh, I know," I said, trying not to appear too excited.

I called an old friend of mine who had gone to Union Theological Seminary, and she gave me the name of a colleague who had recently been ordained in the Metropolitan Community Church, a Protestant denomination dedicated to LGBT-friendly liturgy and worship. This minister, whom I began referring to as Reverend Jen, had been raised in an evangelical home and was now a chaplain at Brown. After our first phone call I knew she was the one: a lesbian who believed in a resurrected Jesus. Who could be better? Because despite my insistence on all I was still entitled to, I wanted a lesbian to perform our wedding. I wanted the person who married us not to just accept or approve of our love affair, but to intimately know its territory, its shadows and its pleasures.

We met with Jen in her office at Brown. She looked to be in her midthirties, with dark hair cut close to her head. She had broad shoulders and an angular face. It was Saturday and she wore a T-shirt and jeans, smelled slightly of mint gum and even more slightly of cigarettes. Her office was sunny and comfortable, with a couch and a few soft chairs, the walls decorated with posters commemorating various interfaith gatherings. After a few minutes of small talk, Jen asked us what we wanted our ceremony to be about, what we wanted it to include.

"Well, I want to use all the strong words," I said. "Marriage, marry, wedding, even wife."

Chris cringed at that last one. She didn't like wife. "Okay, maybe not wife," I said. "But I hate partner, and I really don't like commitment ceremony. It sounds like we're having a ritual to commit each other to an asylum." This is what I didn't say: I want all the things I've always wanted.

Jen asked Chris if there was anything she did or didn't want to be part of our wedding. "I want Bach's cello suites," she said, without hesitation. "And an E. E. Cummings poem." Chris looked at me, smiling. In our early days, she often left E. E. Cummings's lines around my apartment, scribbled them on slips of paper before she left in the morning: *possibly i like the thrill of under me you so quite new.* And: *because I love you)last night.* When we had been together for a few months and she was beginning a new trial, I gave her a pair of earrings as a good-luck present. On the card I wrote: *nobody, not even the rain, has such small ears.*

Chris and I paid for the wedding ourselves, with our own savings. I say our, although in reality the money was Chris's. I made a small graduate student teaching salary and had health benefits, but Chris supported both of us. Even though she had taken an in-house counsel job when we moved to western Massachusetts from Philly, she still made plenty of money. Regardless of Chris's salary, I always worked, always brought in some small amount of income. I taught and worked as a nanny. And in the weeks before we were married, I took a job grading placement exams so that I could buy Chris a painting, which I surprised her with on the morning before our wedding.

In the fall, when we had been engaged for nearly six months, Chris finally called her parents to share the news. "What did they say?" I asked Chris when she came downstairs after the troublingly short phone call.

"Not much," she said in a tight voice. "Not that I'm surprised," she added, and I knew she was trying to sound detached. "Not that I expected anything else."

I knew that an expected disappointment was a disappointment nonetheless. "Maybe you should go there," I suggested. "Not now," I clarified, seeing the alarm on her face. "In a few days. Give them some time to take it in, and then go and have a real conversation about it, face-to-face. I'll go with you, if you want." I hoped this offer sounded more genuine than it was. I didn't want to go with her. I was still a little afraid of her parents.

"I'll think about it," she said.

In the end she went to Worcester without me. I never really knew what happened between Chris and her parents that day. I know that she told them she wanted them in her life, but that her life was changing now. She was getting married. And if they couldn't celebrate that, if they couldn't stand up and offer their love and support, then they could no longer be part of her life. I don't know exactly what they said in response to her ultimatum. I do know that Chris came home late that night and everything about her was different. She came into our dark bedroom, and even though I couldn't see her, even though she didn't speak because she thought I was asleep, I knew what had happened while she was away. The air around her was different then. And in the morning, when I saw her face, when I listened to her tell me that her parents would be at the wedding, there was a new softness around her jaw, around those bones that she had, since I met her, often rubbed in the evenings before sleep, complaining of a soreness that would not go away.

In March, my mother and I went to Neiman Marcus to find my wedding dress. "Wow," my mother said, holding up a black, floor-length gown. "Try this one."

"I don't know," I said. I didn't want a white wedding dress, but I wasn't sure I wanted a black one either.

"It's gorgeous, and it would be perfect on you," my mother said, handing it to me.

She was right. The dress was perfect. Black silk with white piping and a thin, white belt. It was Grace Kelly and Audrey Hepburn; it was elegant and perfect. The store was out of my size, but the saleswoman assured me that she could send for it, that according to her computer there was one in Dallas.

A few days later the saleswoman called. "So I wasn't actually able to find that dress," she said. "But I can give you a full refund."

"But that's my wedding dress!" I cried.

"You bought a black dress for your wedding?" she asked.

I hung up the phone and starting crying. Then I called my friend Stephanie, who worked at Neiman Marcus, and told her that my wedding dress was gone. "Oh, I'll find it," she said. "I'll find that dress." And she did. And when I went to pick it up in Boston the next week, Stephanie gave me a handbag filled with Chanel makeup and brought me to the couture dressing room, where she offered me cookies and champagne.

Chris couldn't decide what to wear to the wedding. Her mother wanted to go shopping with her, but Chris kept putting her off. Finally she sent Chris a picture of a dress from a bridal magazine. "This one would look good with Erin's dress," she wrote next to it. It was a lovely dress, deep-blue silk, two pieces, almost like a suit. But I thought Chris should wear pants. She always wore pants. She said she would think about it.

"While you're thinking about it," I said, "why don't you just go shopping with your mother? She's making a gesture. You should accept it." I wanted her to go shopping with her mother because I didn't want to go shopping with Chris. I didn't want to be responsible for her clothes. Or maybe I did, but I didn't want to overstep what seemed like her decision. If she were a man, I might have bought her wedding suit, might have told her what looked good and what didn't. And I might have also insisted she choose a simple platinum wedding band and not the ring she really wanted, the rough-hewn titanium band made by a friend of hers who also made bicycles. But she was a woman, and because of this I believed she deserved autonomy in matters of aesthetics, and I left those choices up to her.

By April I was, quite honestly, devoting more of my time to wedding planning than I was to my classwork. Chris had virtually no interest in the endless details, and so I did most of the planning with my neighbor Emily, a slight and beautiful woman with a pixie haircut and an impeccable sense of style. Emily was an expert on midcentury furniture and eyeliner and lingerie. Politics meant nothing to her; she once told me she had never voted. But she adamantly supported marriage equality insofar as she believed my wedding was every bit as real as anyone else's. You should register, she insisted. And send engraved invitations. She said yes to the string quartet for the ceremony and yes to the jazz band for the reception. She took me to her hairdresser for a practice run on hairstyles; she advised me on nail polish. Emily was not interested in how my wedding would circumvent the patriarchal power structure. She was interested in getting me to buy two pairs of shoes in case I wanted to change after the ceremony.

And when I would think, as I sometimes did, with a great rush of epiphanic anxiety, *Oh my God, I'm marrying a woman!* Emily would call and say, "What's new with the brides?" And together we would ruminate over details and decisions as though there was nothing more normal in all the world than this lesbian wedding of mine, and I would think, it's true, it's really true: I can have everything I have ever wanted.

Emily had no other gay friends, knew no lesbians other than Chris and me, but was wholehearted in her enthusiasm for us, as was her husband, a foul-mouthed yet affable financier with whom Chris spent many Sunday afternoons, watching sports on his flat-screen TV. We were all pleased and amused by the synchronicity of our coupling. This would often happen with straight couples we were friends with; the man would be taken by Chris's masculinity, by the ways in which she was one of the guys. It was a comfortable arrangement for everyone, this gendered contrast between Chris and me, these ways in which we were just like them. Eventually, though, Chris would surprise these men, eventually the conversation would turn to the wage gap, or girls in Afghanistan, or Madeleine Albright, and suddenly they would remember she was a woman. And they would change the subject, offer her a beer. They would, it seemed, try to forget that even though she was a match for their strength and their confidence, she lived in a different world.

A few months before our wedding, we went to Spain. It was an early honeymoon, because our wedding was planned for September when I would be teaching and unable to get away. In Barcelona, in a gift shop across the street from the Sagrada Família, I bought two flamenco dancer dolls for the top of our wedding cake. Chris and I both thought it was a grandly clever idea, but in the end I decided not to use them. I wasn't ready for the jokes. I was earnest in my efforts and resolute in my beliefs. Which is to say I was very nervous and a little sad. I knew that my future was with Chris, but I didn't honestly know what that meant. This, of course, *is* marriage: we join hands and walk into the unknown, together, but in my case I was also walking into a private unknown, and a future unlike any I had ever dreamed for myself. Hence the perfect flowers and the perfect dress. Hence the flamenco dancers wrapped in tissue paper and packed away in the attic.

This is what I remember about our wedding: It didn't rain. Chris wore a dress, but not the one her mother had chosen for her. I didn't change my shoes for the reception; Chris didn't wear shoes at all. "I'm the father of the bride," Chris's father said to the bartender before the ceremony began. "Can I get a beer?"

The ceremony was on the wooded grounds of an inn, on a stone patio in a grove of pines. A cellist played the Bach suites and also my favorite hymn, "Lord of All Hopefulness." Our friends and family stood for the service, all except my eighty-year-old grandmother and our forty-weeks-pregnant friend, Alisa. Reverend Jen wore a clerical collar and black suit, and she embodied church authority and queerness, and I adored her for both. She spoke so confidently of God's love and of our union that even though there was no assertion of the power vested in her by the state of Massachusetts, it was wonderfully, perfectly clear that a power was vested in her, and we were bound by it.

My sister read an E. E. Cummings poem, not one from our courtship, but another we both loved, one that was a little more about sky and green trees than it was about sex. I married Chris with that ring I didn't like, and she married me with one I had deliberated over for weeks, a ring that she claimed to like, but who knew? It hardly mattered now. We were married.

When the ceremony was over, Chris and I joined hands and turned away from our guests to walk back down the stone path toward the inn. Before we had gone more than a few steps, Chris looked at me and whispered, "My family." And we turned back again. "We forgot something," I said, and everyone laughed as we each walked into the embrace of our own parents. My father kissed my cheeks, my mother smoothed my hair, and I quickly kissed my brother and sister. But Chris's parents held her in a shared embrace for a long time, and then opened their arms for her sisters, and for a moment we all stood and watched.

8 | A Harmonious Match

Y ou know," Chris said, during one of our many conversations about how and when we might start trying to have a baby, "I remember the first time we talked about having kids. I told you that I might not want to, and you said that was fine."

I was entirely certain that conversation never happened. "I would never have said that. Not having children was never fine with me."

"So you would have left me if I had said I definitely didn't want kids?" Chris asked.

Yes, I thought, I would have left you. But I didn't say that. Instead I leaned over and kissed her. "Just think," I said, "when I'm pregnant my boobs will be fantastic."

What I didn't understand then, as I joked and flirted, was that when Chris brought up that old conversation (which I still, to this day, do not remember), she was asking me to confirm my loyalty, and also her primacy. She was asking me to want her more than I wanted anyone else. More than I wanted a baby.

But in truth I didn't want anyone more than I wanted a baby. I didn't say this out loud, or at least I hardly ever said it out loud. But it was true. Occasionally the longing overwhelmed me with its urgency, its bright greed, but mostly it was an even wanting; it was the single drop of methylene blue that turned every cell wall, every nucleus, a coppery indigo. It was the gold coin hidden in my pocket, heavy and warm in my fingers.

My desire for a baby was oversized. It was preoccupying. It wasn't great for my career, or my marriage. I knew all those things, but I didn't care. My desire for a baby felt like an inalienable part of me, and it seemed if Chris loved me as she did, then surely she didn't mind the force of it; surely I did not need to temper it for her sake.

Chris didn't want children in the same way I did; she had not, in fact, planned on having them. But I attributed this to the reality of growing up gay in the seventies and eighties. She knew she wouldn't have a husband, so then how would she have children? She could not have imagined becoming a non-gestating, non-lactating, married-to-a-woman, lesbian mom. She couldn't have imagined becoming a mother and still remaining herself.

But now the lesbian baby boom was well underway, and couples were using sperm donors and artificial insemination to grow their families with relative ease. And while second-parent adoption (the legal extension of parental rights to the nonbiological parent) was legal in only a few states, Massachusetts was one of them. I was certain we could—and would—have children. I felt fertile; we could afford the cost. And like getting married, having a baby was something to which I still felt entirely, inherently, entitled

In the fall, after our wedding, I joined a mentoring organization called Sisters Inc., which paired women with tween girls, whom we referred to as our little sisters. We all gathered once a month for an art workshop with a girl-power theme, and then got together in pairs a few other times each month to do something fun. The women in the group were artists and musicians, bakers and potters. Some rode horses with their little sisters; others taught theirs to play guitar and drums. Most of the little sisters were from multigenerational rural families; their parents and grandparents were sheep and maple-syrup farmers, lumbermen. My little sister's parents were in jail, and she lived with a foster family in town. Allie was one of the oldest girls in Sisters Inc., but she seemed like the youngest. She was outspoken and earnest, and spoke with a drawl whose origins I could not place. She concentrated deeply on the monthly art projects and went back for third and fourth helpings of the snack.

Allie didn't want to play music or ride horses when we were together, which was lucky because I could do neither. She wanted to knit, which I taught her to do, and go to the movies. She also liked to go to Walmart. I hated Walmart, but I took her anyway. I bought her markers and paper, yarn for her knitting, and goldfish crackers. Chris and I lived a few blocks from Allie's school, and some afternoons she walked to our house and did her homework at our dining room table. I often fed her an early dinner, rich and comforting foods like chicken pot pie, which Chris and I both loved but didn't often make for ourselves. Allie's grandparents, with whom she lived until she entered the foster care system, were fundamentalist Christians, but Allie seemed entirely unconcerned that I was married to a woman. She asked me if we were going to have kids. I told her I hoped so. "Two moms!" she said, shaking her head in disbelief. "That's going to be so cool."

One night, after Allie had left and we were getting ready for bed, I asked Chris if she would ever consider adopting a child from foster care. She thought about it for a moment and then said, "I would, I think."

"One as old as Allie?" I asked.

"Maybe," she said.

"But you miss out on so much," I said, as though Chris were the one trying to convince me of something. "And there's so much you can't control."

"I think when you decide to adopt, it's not really about what you can control. It's about loving a child."

I stayed quiet then, because anything I said would make me sound like a terrible person. I didn't want to adopt Allie, or any other child. I couldn't forsake my dream of motherhood through physical transformation or, quite honestly, my need for control.

When we got into bed, I said, "I really don't want to adopt."

"I know," Chris said.

"I want to be pregnant, and give birth, and nurse, all those things."

"I think you will," she said.

I didn't ask Chris if she also wanted to be pregnant and to give birth. I knew she didn't. I had asked her once, many years ago, but even then the question was only a formality. If you had asked me on that first night I met her if she wanted to be pregnant, I would have told you no, absolutely not. There was something entirely contained about Chris's body. There was no space in her for another beating heart. And I am sure that her desire for containment, which the animal in me saw as compatible with my desire to grow another human in my body, was one of the reasons I was drawn to her, and one of the reasons she was drawn to me. We are taught the ancient complexities of mating, that men and women's bodies are designed to sense a virile mate, a hospitable womb. What we are not taught, but what I believe to be true, is that even two women can sense the possibility of a harmonious match.

Sisters Inc. was a feminist organization whose roots and mission were essentially political: empowerment through mentorship and the arts. The executive director was a young lesbian named Kelly who had recently emigrated from Brooklyn. Kelly was a women's historian and archivist. Her partner, Gaby, a botanist, was also a Sisters Inc. mentor. On their fridge there was a magnet that said *Cats Not Kids*, which was clearly a relic from their past, as when I met them Gaby was six months pregnant with their first child.

Kelly was the first lesbian I had ever known who was like me, who cared about eyebrow waxing and cookware, who read Ann Patchett novels and shelter magazines. Her hair always looked fantastic, her makeup perfect. Her laugh was contagious; her high-heel collection was epic. She had gorgeous dresses and lovely dishes and threw the best parties. Her politics were radical and fervent and a little intimidating. She was startlingly confident. I knew from the first time we met I wanted to be her friend.

Gaby and Kelly's baby, a boy due in late spring, was conceived with sperm from a friend of theirs. A known donor. He would be their baby's father, they told us, although not in the way you are thinking. They were making a new kind of family, they told Chris and me one evening when we had them over for dinner to ask them all our baby-making questions. A new family without models, without set roles. "I mean, if you looked at us, you wouldn't expect me to be the bio mom," Gaby said. And it was true: I would have assumed Kelly would, like me, want to carry their child. But Kelly was repulsed by even the idea of pregnancy, while Gaby had always believed she would have a child, despite her butchness.

We asked them about their donor, and they told us their sweet conception story, and that a known donor was essential to them, that their beliefs about the meaning of family and a child's sense of identity demanded total transparency and connection.

Chris and I didn't really say much in response, and I changed the topic of conversation to baby names. Later, after they had left, Chris asked me, cautiously, what I thought about using a known donor. I told her I would be okay with it if we knew the right person, but I couldn't imagine who that person might be. She said she couldn't do it. "He could change his mind at any time during the pregnancy," she said.

"Well, we'd get him to sign something."

"But he could get out of anything he signed. He could change his mind anytime, and he can't legally renounce rights until after birth."

Neither one of us had any idea who this "he" was, but still we kept on. "Well, we wouldn't do it with someone we didn't trust entirely," I said.

"I don't trust anyone entirely," Chris said.

I laughed, but I knew she wasn't kidding. As a lawyer and the daughter of a cop, Chris didn't really believe in the innate goodness of humanity.

"So if we use an anonymous donor, have you thought of what sort of characteristics would matter to you?" I asked.

"I want someone who looks like me," she said. "I mean, not exactly like me, but the same general ethnicity, Lithuanian, Swedish."

"I'm not sure we'll be able to find that particular combination."

"You know what I mean."

"You mean not Asian."

"Is that bad?"

"Oh no," I said, although it was hard not to sense the racist overtones of our conversation. "You want someone who looks like you," I said. "So do I."

I also wanted to choose an identity-release donor, a donor who was willing to be contacted by our children when they were eighteen. Chris wasn't so sure. "Really?" she asked.

"It's a door," I said, trying to sound equanimous, "and we have to give it to our kids, even if they never open it. They have to know it's there."

Later Chris would thank me for my insistence on that point, but in truth she was the one who deserved thanks. My claim on our theoretical children was much stronger than hers then, and it was easier for me to suggest that such a thing might be necessary. She was the vulnerable one, and she agreed anyway.

Chris didn't want to sort through donor profiles with me, so I told her I would do the early research and show her the top picks, as though I were her donor-selection intern. This was in the early days of the internet, and we still had dial-up; I still had to plug my laptop into the beeping modem and listen to the shrill call of one machine to another before I could go to the sperm bank's website and see what new donors might be waiting for me there.

Chris also wasn't interested in interviewing doctors or midwives, or even in reading Rachel Pepper's *Ultimate Guide to Pregnancy for Lesbians*. "Can you just summarize?" she asked me when I gave her the book.

I looked at her. "Can you please just read it?"

And so she did; she read it cover to cover one Saturday afternoon. "Interesting," she said. "Seems pretty straightforward."

I asked her if she had read the section about the challenges of insemination, including the short life span of thawed sperm and the possibility of expensive fertility treatment. "You're not even thirty yet," Chris said. "She's not talking about you." And while I needed Chris's confidence and her healthy perspective, part of me wanted her to share in my obsession—the part of me that mistook obsession for interest, for engagement. But the baby was an abstraction to Chris, and she approached the process of getting one as something that seemed possible, and logical. The data showed that it had worked for many people; why wouldn't it work for us?

So I obsessed without her, and I turned the baby into a to-do list. There were many decisions to make: Did we want "washed" sperm that could be directly inserted into my uterus by a doctor or midwife, or sperm that was hearty enough to swim through my cervix so we could do the inseminations ourselves? (Definitely not. We could barely load the dishwasher together.) Did we want to use Gaby and Kelly's lesbian obstetrician or the midwifery practice I had been hearing about, the one that made insemination house calls? Every day I made more phone calls and downloaded new donor profiles. I began to chart my cycle. I liked the forward motion of my to-do list, and for a little while I was content to busy myself with these tasks, but before long there were glitches, small complications in my well-ordered system. A donor we loved was suddenly no longer available; my limited graduate student insurance didn't cover the house-call midwives, and Chris's insurance, which did cover the midwives, was not available to domestic partners. I waited and waited to ovulate and impatiently stood by while day 14, day 15, day 16 passed without so much as a twinge in my side.

In early spring I made an appointment with Gaby's obstetrician. Dr. Marshall was tall and blonde, boyish in a New England prep school way. At that first consultation she told me she herself could not imagine wanting to be pregnant. This strikes me now as an odd and inappropriate disclosure, but at the time it barely registered. I was just glad she enjoyed the professional challenge of getting other lesbians pregnant, which she did with an impressive success rate. We chatted for a little while, and then she asked me about my cycle. Was it regular? I showed her a small chart I had been keeping, whose template I had photocopied from the back of *Taking Charge of Your Fertility*. The paper was soft from being folded so many times, and nearly every box was filled with letters and abbreviations written in different shades of ink. I had taken note of basal body temperature, changes in cervical mucus, bloating, breast tenderness, cycle length. Dr. Marshall looked at the chart in disbelief. "You didn't need to do this," she said. She was trying—with limited success—to keep from laughing. "I think you need to get a hobby," she said.

Why didn't I—after that humiliating and cruel remark—just thank Dr. Marshall for her time and leave? Because I needed her. Gaby and Kelly said she was the best, and I had read too many stories of incompetent doctors, doctors who didn't understand how insemination with thawed sperm really worked or who refused to do weekend and evening inseminations. So I stayed. My staying was the seed of both my resignation and my grief, although it would be the grief that bloomed faster, sunk deeper roots. It would be the grief that I would continue to mistake as well-justified and understandable worry, as necessary vigilance, when really what I felt was a terrible sadness that despite what I still believed I was entitled to, I would not, could not, conceive a baby in my bed with the person I loved.

I asked Dr. Marshall the rest of my questions and thanked her for her time and told her I would be in touch when we were ready to begin inseminations. When Chris called to ask how the consult had gone, I said, "Oh, it was good. I liked her. You will too."

A few days after my visit to Dr. Marshall, my neighbor Emily called me and asked me to come over; she had some news. She was pregnant. They weren't exactly trying, but they were thrilled. She was tired, and the world smelled terrible, and she couldn't get enough cookies. "Cookies and naps!" Emily said cheerfully. "That's my new life."

How exciting! I said. How amazing that you weren't even trying! How amazing. I stayed long enough not to seem rude, and then I walked across the street as quickly as I could, trying my best not to cry before I got to my front door. It was not envy I felt so much as embarrassment, and shame. I thought of my chart. I took it out of my purse and unfolded it. My face burned at the sight of all those letters, all those tiny parentheticals, the occasional smiley face. *You need to get a hobby.* I tore up the chart into tiny pieces and threw them in the kitchen garbage. I went upstairs to our bedroom and threw away my basal body thermometer. Then I went downstairs to start dinner and tried not to look out the window at the lights in Emily's kitchen, and the lights in the room down the hall, which, she had told me, would be the baby's.

Trust 9

After a few months of negative pregnancy tests I began to lose my mind. A friend of my mother's sent me a smooth, black river stone painted with the word "trust." In the accompanying note she told me that the rock would get darker and more beautiful as the oils from my fingers smoothed its surface. I kept the rock by my bedside table and every morning I held it, took a few semideep breaths, and pretended to meditate on its message. Then I jumped out of bed and ran to the bathroom, where I peed on a thin plastic strip, inserted it into my battery-operated ovulation monitor, and breathed shallow breaths while I waited for the day's reading.

The machine needed a few minutes to read the tea leaves of my urine, minutes during which I stood with my back to its blinking face. I looked out the window at the narrow river across the street, and beyond it to the town's one-room library, whose etched cornerstones reminded me that Wise Men Put Up Knowledge. Over the months I used that monitor I must have spent hours at that window waiting for the monitor to beep, fantasizing about the day when would I walk next to the river with my baby, then bathe her in the claw-foot tub beside me, leaning over its curved ceramic lip to soap her body. When the monitor finally beeped I would grab for it, only to have it tell me in its own indifferent way, not yet. And then, in an instant, the baby would vanish from the tub. On those mornings I longed for the chance to walk out of that bathroom and into an entirely different life. A life in which I slid back into bed with a man to whom I could whisper: *Not today, but why don't we try anyway?*

You need a mantra," a friend told me when I confided my anxiety. "I use them all the time. Try one like, 'All will be well, all manner of things will be well.'"

But all was not well, I wanted to point out to her, and if I didn't get pregnant soon, all would most certainly not be well. I feared this concept of wellness, as though, baby or not, the universe would continue in its indifferent divinity and I would make my way in it; I would learn hard lessons and be tempered by loss and bloom into full personhood. That all sounded lovely and maybe I would get on board later but right now my stakes were too high.

Still, a mantra was not a bad idea. "I've got a mantra," I told my mother on the phone when we were talking, as we often were, about my not being pregnant. "Oh good," she said. "What is it?"

"Jesus has my baby."

My mother burst into laughter.

"Are you laughing at my mantra?"

"No, no," she said, still laughing. "I love it, you know I do."

I knew she did. I loved it too, although more than anything I was surprised by it. Jesus was mostly in the shadows of my life then. I hadn't chosen Hector's solitary path to God and while I still thought of myself as a faithful person, I had no idea how to act like one. I hadn't been a Catholic long enough to say I was now lapsed, but I was certainly drifting. Occasionally I went to Mass at St. Mary's in Northampton, and I found some joy there, at the familiarity of the service and the sanctuary itself: the stained glass windows, the gently curving arm of each pew, Jesus on the cross, the statues of Mary and the saints tucked into alcoves and window wells.

At St. Mary's I often found a sweet spot of refuge from the noisy world, although there was always an accompanying agitation. There was always the pang of what I had not done, an accounting of the ways I had grown my life according to my own will, and not waited patiently to discern God's. God had become a sort of long-distance benefactor, a patron whom I had disappointed and whose letters, out of shame, I did not open, not realizing that the disappointment was my own. And Jesus, well, he was like a dear friend set out on a long journey, so that weeks sometimes went by without my thinking of him, although when I did it was with genuine fondness, and with longing.

But when I had closed my eyes and coached myself to think of a mantra, I immediately saw Jesus, saw my baby's head against that worn flannel shirt. And I heard him too, heard him laugh at the thought of what I had asked him to do, but still opening his arms to do it.

On that one blessed day each month when my ovulation predictor deigned to illuminate its blinking, purple egg, I called Dr. Marshall's office and told the receptionist to put me on the morning schedule, crossing my fingers in hope that Dr. Marshall herself would be out of the office. As it turned out, I far preferred her colleague, Dr. Bryant, a shy but charming Irishman and father of five children. After the first few inseminations, Chris and I had gone straight home to have sex. But soon enough I admitted to myself that I didn't want to have sex after having a speculum in my vagina, and, sometimes, an extraordinarily painful clamp around the lip of my cervix. So we started going to movies, and eventually we just went back to work. And while Chris did not complain about lack of concentration on those workdays, after an insemination I walked through campus cautious and altered, then stood in front of my class and lectured about Emily Dickinson's use of the em dash, thinking only of the two possible outcomes of my morning: a miracle, or nothing at all.

During what fertility experts refer to as the TWW (the two-week wait between insemination and a discernable pregnancy), my body became like the plot of the Sierra Nevada forest I spent a high school summer surveying, cataloging every plant, catching every flying squirrel, holding their squirming bodies in a thick leather glove and tagging their small ears so that later I could break apart owl scat and find those tags. Only when it came to my body, I could see less; what bloomed or withered, divided or didn't, did so in the darkness of a space I couldn't see during a moment I could not be certain of. I could only measure small tremors and tracks, subtle swells of mood and skin. I couldn't be sure of anything other than the blood of failure, and even that came so quietly that the first moment of every sighting took me by surprise.

I told Chris about my mantra. "Does it help?" she asked.

I wanted to snap at her, say that nothing really helped, and nothing ever would, except a baby. But I knew she was tired of my pessimism, tired of my vigilance. I worried she could sense how often I wished for the chance to shed my skin, to enter another life.

"It does help," I said. "Sometimes."

"You know," she said. "I do wish I could get you pregnant."

I touched her face. "Oh, I know you do," I said. I wanted so much for her to not feel responsible, to not feel inadequate, despite the fact that lately I couldn't help myself from seeing her that way.

Chris and I didn't talk about my mantra again, although my mother, as is her way and the way of all my family, kept the humor of it alive. "Good thing Jesus has the baby," my mother said as we carried boxes into my sister's new apartment on a warm afternoon in May. "Because I couldn't do this lifting without you."

By midsummer I had become increasingly bothered by the peeling lead paint on the windowsills and sashes of our two-hundred-year-old house. "I think I'll ask the owner about the lead paint," I said to Chris one day. "I'll tell her we're trying to have a baby, and we need her to fix it."

"You mean have the house abated?"

"No," I said. "I'll ask her to paint over the windows."

"I'm not a real estate lawyer, but I'm pretty sure that's illegal, once it's been determined that there's lead."

"Well, we can't have a baby in a house with lead paint."

"I know," Chris said, calmly. "All I'm saying is that I don't know if she's going to fix it."

A few days after I wrote to the owner, she wrote back, telling me she had decided to sell the house. It turned out Chris, despite not being a real estate lawyer, was right. Once I raised the issue of lead paint, the owner was obligated by law to abate, but she was going to sell instead. "You can either buy the house, or you can move," she wrote.

There was no way we were going to buy the house. It was charming and grand, but there was a spring below the foundation and who knows how many other hidden and expensive quirks. We started looking for a new house and the question of where we would live quickly became the question of how we would live. Would we buy a more expensive house in town with the assumption that I would work after the baby was born and help pay the mortgage? Or would we move further into the country—the hill-towns, as they were called in western Massachusetts—so that we could buy a less expensive house and live closer to Chris's job if she would be working and I wouldn't?

I had a both ardent and vague assumption that I would stay home with our baby (ardent in that I couldn't imagine not staying home, vague in that I had no real idea of what staying home would be like). Chris wanted to work after we had a baby, but said she would rather not hire a nanny or put our baby in full-time childcare. "I want our kid to be with you," she said, "if you want to stay home." She was always careful then to be diplomatic about our parenting future, careful to let me know that it was fine if I worked and fine if I didn't, but that she herself would be working. Full-time.

And so we decided to begin looking for a house in the hills, although I did not seriously consider what it meant to move so far away from the university where I worked and could work again, should I decide I wanted to. I didn't consider the distance to grocery stores and the bank, to the houses of my friends. I didn't consider much: I was a woman in search of a nest.

In the weeks after I received that letter from our landlord, I woke early to work on my thesis, then spent the afternoons driving through the green hills in search of real estate. I often stopped at small farms to pick fruit, or at unmarked turnoffs where I scrambled down rocks to cold and shaded swimming holes. That summer I also began to swim long distances across a lake I had found on the way to one of my many disappointing house tours. The lake had a small and nearly always empty beach from which I could swim, without a swimming suit, the rhythmic and even strokes that had comforted me since I was a girl.

I never bathed a baby in that claw-foot bathtub. In the fall we bought a house next to a different river. Now our street was a dirt road, and I looked out on a small herd of cows instead of a library. When we had lived there for two weeks a miracle took place inside my body. Two weeks later the miracle revealed itself to me in the form of a faint pink line. So faint, in fact, that I called the pregnancy test consumer help line to ask if it counted as a positive. It did. As I moved through the maddeningly slow and sick weeks of early pregnancy, I no longer needed my mantra. The baby was no bigger than—what was it the books told me?—a comma, a peanut, a kidney bean, but she had a heart and its racing beat became all the mantra I needed. *Thanks so much,* I might have said to Jesus if I weren't so distracted by prenatal vitamin prescriptions and antinausea lollipops, if the vision of him holding my baby hadn't faded like last week's dream. *I can take it from here.*

Trust

10 | Grace

When I was pregnant and baby names the topic of daily conversation, Chris was insistent that, if the baby were a girl, we would call her Grace. I preferred Ruby. I tried to convince Chris by using the name in scenarios that I knew she would like. "Okay, listen to this," I would say, and then, in an enthusiastic yet failed impersonation of a sports announcer, I would call, "Shortstop Ruby Mae!" But Chris would not be swayed. In my heart I knew that Grace was a better name than Ruby; I knew that Ruby was cheekier and trendier than either of us. And Grace was a better match with Chris's last name, which we had already decided to give the baby. "My genes, your name," I had said early in the pregnancy, and while Chris had offered hyphenation, I wasn't interested. I wanted to keep it simple. And I wanted the baby to have something that belonged entirely to Chris.

But I was having trouble letting go of Ruby. It was unusual, while Grace seemed to be everywhere. "Look," I would say, pointing to the personalized towels in the Pottery Barn Kids catalog, "Grace, Dylan, and Madison," and I would slowly shake my head with the danger, the seriousness of it all. "Not great company." But Chris didn't care about towels. "Grace under pressure," she always said. "She's going to need it."

We lived in different worlds during those months of pregnancy and naming babies. I lived in the world of the one child who swam in my belly and whose existence was original and private. Chris lived in the world of the thousands of children who were born each day, the vast majority of them to a mother and a father. So when she said that our daughter would need to be graceful under pressure, she meant that our daughter would be different from the children around her, and she would need grace to navigate those differences. Before we tried to conceive I might have agreed with her. But then I did conceive, and my claim on the child inside my body was utterly personal and my dominion over her was absolute. Hate and politics would not touch her; I would see to that.

My pregnancy, which was so desired and so long-anticipated, was much harder than I had expected. I had been terribly sick in the beginning, which Chris found distressing. In pregnancy I became a much more embodied person, which is to say that I talked about my sore hips, and I talked about my heartburn, and I needed four pillows when I slept. Before it had been her body that we talked about, her stiff shoulder, her cramps, her suspicious mole in need of inspection. This reversal, and, essentially, her displacement, was unsettling. Her response to my nausea, to my new sensitivities and endless need for sleep, reminded me of my high school boyfriend's disappointed surprise when he took me mountain biking and I got so frustrated I threw my bike in a bush. "You're the one girl I thought could handle this," he said, riding on without me.

Chris was much more understanding than my boyfriend had been, but still I knew she had not expected my constant complaining about this pregnancy that I had wanted for so long. She thought I would be a tougher pregnant person, take it more in stride. To make matters worse, friends and acquaintances were often telling me how lucky I was to be married to a woman; surely she rubbed my swollen feet each night, listened attentively to my daily recital of discomfort and worry. "She's probably about as attentive as your husband," I told them.

Because I had an anterior placenta, which meant it was essentially a barrier between the baby and my belly, I could feel the baby move but Chris couldn't. "He's moving!" I would say, and then quickly grab Chris's hand and put it on the spot where I felt the kick. Chris would keep her hand there for a little while, then shake her head. Nothing.

༄

That spring when we were waiting for our baby we were also waiting for the Massachusetts Legislature's response to the state supreme court ruling on gay marriage. In November 2003, when I was pregnant but did not yet know that I was, the court issued a decision stating that restrictions on gay marriage were unconstitutional, a ruling that would make Massachusetts the first state in the nation to legalize gay marriage. On the day the court decision was released, Chris called me from work. I was at home, getting ready for class. "We won!" she said. "I've got the decision, and we won! And you won't believe this language. You just won't believe it." I could tell she had been crying. "Listen to this," she said, reading from the court's decision, "'Limiting the protections, benefits, and obligations of civil marriage to opposite-sex couples violates the basic premises of individual liberty and equality under law.'"

"Oh, that's amazing!" I said. "I'm so happy!" I had to stop myself from adding "for you." I felt like a bystander in the struggle for marriage equality, even though I stood to gain so much from it. When Chris read to me from the decision that day, and later when I read it myself in its entirety, there was a newsreel in my mind: the Stonewall riots, the AIDS quilt on the National Mall, women in Lavender Menace T-shirts. I thought of Minnie Bruce Pratt, and how she lost her children (*her children!*) because she loved women and loving women was a crime. I couldn't stop thinking about how strange it was that I—who had marched in exactly two gay pride parades—would be among the very first lesbians to be legally married. It was a gain I didn't deserve to celebrate. But more than that—and more troubling than that—it was a gain I didn't want. Because if the state now said we could be married, then what had we been? Secretly I found the decision embarrassing—it forced me to admit that I wasn't equal in the eyes of the government, or the culture, and that it would take a supreme court decision and a legislative act, not just a perfect wedding, to make me so.

"This will be big for us," Chris often said in the months that followed the supreme court decision, when she read something about it in the paper, or talked it over with friends. "Even though no one really knows what it will mean," she said, "it will be big. Especially for our kid."

I would smile then and murmur my agreement, my shared anticipation. But in truth I didn't agree. I didn't like the idea of the state of Massachusetts having anything to do with my child's life. Rights granted were rights that could be taken away, and I couldn't bear the idea that the life of this leaping bean inside me—invisible and beloved and mine—would be subject to the whims of government, of strangers who believed their opinions were more essential than her, and her mothers', humanity.

There was a reason, a real reason, I did not want to name our daughter Grace, and it had to do with Catholicism and with Hector, and with a God I no longer knew. When I got pregnant I stopped going to Mass entirely. I told myself I felt too vulnerable to the Catholic Church's hostile politics, that I was disgusted by the active role the Church was playing in the fight against marriage equality. And I was vulnerable, although not only because of the church's homophobia. I could still hear Hector's voice inside my head, telling me that I simply could not have both God and Chris. And not only had I chosen Chris, but I had promised myself to her, and together we were going to have a child. I couldn't keep myself from wondering what Hector would think of me now. He lingered as a presence of profound understanding but also disregard, and so it was impossible for me to discern which of our shared findings I could still claim as true. I knew that Hector didn't have the definitive word on God; I knew that it would be possible—somehow—to untangle the thread of my belief from his, but I didn't want to. It was easier, or so it seemed, to just turn away.

In those days I thought that Chris was engaged in a fight that was hers, and it was about being seen, about her life and love having equal value in this world, and I believed that it was not my fight. And maybe it wasn't my fight. But I also believed that I didn't have a fight at all, which wasn't true. I had once put the entirety of my trust in someone and he had betrayed me; he told me that I could not have the life I wanted and the woman I loved. And because Hector explained me to myself in a way that no else had, before or since, I could not fully admit his betrayal.

I thought of homophobia then as something grievous and stark: I thought of men dying alone because their partners couldn't keep vigil at their hospital bedsides, and of teenagers who lived on the streets because they were kicked out of their evangelical homes. I did not yet understand that homophobia can also be a small and pervasive anguish. It can be people we trust telling us we want the wrong things, that we are the wrong sort of people. And they tell us in particular and complex and intimate ways, ways that make it difficult to justify our affection for them, but just as difficult to relinquish it. We become the child who is set down again after being spun by her arms: we know there is a floor below us because we can see it, but it doesn't feel the way it once did.

I had fulfilled Hector's prophecy. I surrendered God, and the Church. Although it is not entirely accurate to say that I surrendered. I didn't acknowledge then that I was in a losing battle. I wanted no part of battles; I had no interest in the fight.

Every night I crawled into bed with *Ina May's Guide to Childbirth* and a tube of Mustela stretch-mark cream. And every morning I woke early to practice yoga and drink smoothies and check the baby's developmental progress on babycenter.com. I was no Dorothy Day and I no longer thought I should be. There was a baby growing in my body, and soon that baby would be in my arms. Soon that baby would have a name, a name that was, a friend reminded me when I told her I was partial to Ruby, the one lasting gift that was mine to give this child.

One weekend when we were visiting Chris's family, her mother asked Chris why she didn't want to be pregnant. "I never have," Chris said, entirely unapologetically. "It doesn't interest me."

"But don't you want to experience what Erin is experiencing? Don't you want that connection to your baby?" I knew she was talking about a genetic connection, not the fleeting physical connection of pregnancy.

"Nope," Chris said.

Later, when we were driving home, I told Chris I thought her mother really wanted her to be having this baby.

"You think?" she said, laughing.

"It must be strange for her," I said, "that you're about to become a mother but you're not pregnant." I thought of how pleased my own mother must have felt that I was the pregnant one.

"I don't really think of myself as about to become a mother," Chris said. "You're going to be the mother, not me."

"What are you going to be then?"

"A parent, but not exactly a mother. I've been thinking I want a name for myself that isn't Mom."

I settled back into the reclined car seat. "Okay," I said. "I'm sure we can think of something." I was happy, relieved even, that Chris didn't think of herself as a mother. I did, and like the role of bride—only much more so—I was grateful to keep it for myself.

In the days and weeks after Chris and I had that conversation, people started asking Chris what the baby was going to call her.

"Ma'am," she said.

One evening I asked Chris what she really wanted our child to call her. "Let's see what mother is in Lithuanian," I suggested, opening my computer. After a few minutes of searching I found it. "Motina," I said, with as much composure as I could muster.

Chris laughed.

"It's sort of a maternal version of Christina," I said, "which is nice."

She was still laughing.

"Okay, okay," I said, closing the computer. "Not Motina."

A few weeks later our friends Darius and Alisa were over and we asked them for suggestions. Darius had two moms, although they had gotten together when Darius was four years old, so he called his other mom Judy. "How about Mati?" Darius asked. "I knew some kids who called their mom that. I think it's Thai for mother."

"I like it," Chris said. "Mati. It has a great sound."

"We've never been to Thailand," I pointed out.

"But we like Thai food," Chris said.

"And that's what we'll tell our kid when she asks why she calls you Mati?"

Chris shrugged. "There are stranger reasons."

I wasn't sure I agreed with her, but I didn't say anything. It was her decision. And besides, I loved Mati. It was sweet and short, and it suited Chris perfectly. And it still left Mother and all its derivatives for me.

Many years later, when not one but two children called Chris

Mati, we would learn that it was not Thai for mother. It was Croatian.

In the early spring, Chris boarded a bus to Boston to attend a day of protest at the legislature. The legislature had been given 180 days to make the supreme court's marriage equality ruling a reality, and now a constitutional convention, the state's first in a decade, was attempting to garner support for an amendment banning gay marriage.

"I don't think I'll go with you," I told Chris when she said she was taking the day off to go to the convention.

"Probably smart," she said. "It's going to be intense."

I was seven months pregnant then and I could not see the fundamentalists. I could not bear the yelling. I knew that if I saw the hate unfold in real time I would be terrified. I knew that I would also be annoyed. I listened to the protesting on the radio, I saw the newspaper photos of people who had come north on buses from as far away as Missouri and Tennessee, and I wanted to tell them all to fuck off. My feet hurt, I wanted to say, and I can't figure out how to install this car seat. The end of civilization as we know it might be coming, but it won't be because of me.

Chris was more resilient to the hate, and also more vulnerable to the possibility of elation. If there would be something to celebrate, then she wanted to be part of it. And so she went and she held her own sign, she held her ground as the hateful crowd tried to push her from her spot in the capitol rotunda. The next morning we lay together in bed and Chris told me stories about young children, no older than five or six, holding signs that said, "One Woman One Man God's Plan," and people praying fervently in English and Spanish.

As I listened I understood that Chris had gone to Boston for the baby. She did not care about prenatal vitamins or birthing center tours or cribs; she didn't care how many grams of protein I had eaten that day. She believed in a different kind of vigilance and preparation. The trouble was I couldn't admit that our child would need what Chris was fighting for. Her fight suggested that all three of us were vulnerable in a way I couldn't bear. I pulled her hand further over my stomach, matching her palm to the baby's floating rump, in yet another attempt at helping the two of them make a physical connection. "I'm glad you're back," I told her, and I turned to kiss her face. "I'm glad it's over."

In early May it was decided that the legislature's proposed amendment and ballot measure were not enough to stay the court's decision, and that marriage licenses would be available to gay and lesbian couples. Chris wanted to get our license right away; we needed to get married before the baby arrived. I agreed, but still I dragged my feet. We were already married. But the truth was, legally speaking, we weren't, and we needed and wanted the legal benefits of marriage. And we wanted to be part of history. Even I had to admit I wanted that. So we went to the town hall and filed for a license. The clerk was cheerful and kind and, in her reserved New England way, genuinely pleased to give us what we needed. I called Steve, the minister at the country church where we occasionally attended services, and asked him if he would perform the ceremony.

"But you know," I said after he told me it would be his pleasure, "we're already married."

"I know," Steve said.

"So I don't want another wedding," I said.

"So we'll make it something else."

Steve came to our house in the early evening, sweetly dressed in a linen jacket and blue button-up shirt. Before we began the brief ceremony he drank a glass of water and told us a story about Dot Mason, the woman who had lived in our house for generations.

We went into the living room, made a few jokes about my bare feet and pregnant belly, and began. Steve read a reworking of the first Psalm, changing "a tree planted near streams of water" to "two women resting near a river." He asked us to make promises to each other, and as I repeated the words he slowly offered me, not the vows we had written and recited two years ago, but new vows, I was filled with an uncomplicated happiness. The room was bright in the summer evening. Chris said her new vows, holding my hand, reaching over to put her other hand on my belly. I rode the minutes of that brief ceremony the way my children would someday ride the small open-car train at the park—their hesitation and dread giving way to the joyful understanding that not only was this nothing to fear, it was something unexpectedly perfect, and over much too soon.

∞✧∞

In truth I loved no name more than I loved Grace. In the week before my due date, when every part of me seemed to be softening under the heat of the August sun, when every anxiety—even the anxiety of labor—started to loosen its hold on me, I woke one morning and the name was the first thing that came into my mind, and it did not frighten me.

"I think the baby's a boy," I said to Chris that afternoon, "but if it's a girl, I think we should name her Grace."

Chris nodded, and I knew she was trying not to show her excitement. "Sounds good," she said.

"But I think it's a boy," I said.

"I know you do."

The baby was a girl.

And it was the nurse, clipboard in hand, who first asked for her name.

"Grace," Chris said and looked at me. "Right?"

"Right," I said in dreaming disbelief that we had a girl child to name, that the boy child I felt certain of was nothing but an idea. After the nurse left I called my friend Karin to tell her that the baby had arrived. "It's a girl and her name is Grace," I said.

"Well," Karin said, "the Grace of God."

The Grace of God. Would such a thing ever again roll so easily off my tongue? I tilted my head and raised my shoulder to cradle the phone so that I could touch the baby's birth-flushed face. "She is," I said. "She absolutely is."

We held Grace all that night in the hospital. Chris lay beside me on a cot the night nurse brought in, and we whispered to each other and passed the baby between us. Sometime before dawn, I fell asleep with Grace tucked beside me like a hot water bottle. When morning came exhaustion began to creep in, but suddenly there was so much to do: hearing tests, nursing consultations, heel pricks. As we were packing up, a gray-haired woman in a suit and wire-rimmed glasses came into the room with the paperwork for Grace's birth certificate. Our attorney had told us that when Chris legally adopted Grace two months after her birth we would be given a final birth certificate, but a preliminary one still had to be filed, and it would have only my name on it. But then same-sex marriage became legal in Massachusetts and no one knew what the decision meant for children born into these marriages. Chris began filling out the form, and when she got to the line for father's name, she said, "What should I write here?"

The woman took the clipboard from Chris and looked down at it over her glasses. "Well, look at that," she said, smiling. "This is my first baby with two moms since the ruling, so"—she paused for a moment and looked over the form—"I think we should cross out father, and you should write your name." She looked at Chris. "I'll type in your name." She nodded, tapping the clipboard emphatically. "That's what we'll do. We worked hard for this, we waited a long time, so let's just do it!"

Chris and I looked at each other. We? Chris smiled at me, and then she took back the clipboard and finished filling out the form. Later, when I asked Chris if she thought that woman was a lesbian, she said she didn't think so. "But how can you know?" I asked. Chris thought about it for a second. "She looked just like my kindergarten teacher, Mrs. Cuppenheimer," she said. "And Mrs. Cuppenheimer was *not* gay."

My parents were with us in the hospital room that morning, and a few months later my father would tell everyone at the Christmas dinner table that our encounter with the birth certificate woman was the moment when he knew that his granddaughter was going to be fine. When I heard him say that, heard him tell the story with tears in his eyes, I was struck by how careful he had been to keep his worries to himself. I made the choice to marry Chris and have a child with her because my father—both my parents—had long insisted that this world was mine to live in without fear and, if necessary, in defiance of the social expectations that confined me. But while that might have been the world my parents offered to me and my siblings, it was not the world they were born into. My father's world still had plenty of room for worry. Of course mine did too, despite how hard I tried to push it away. I was nursing Grace at the Christmas dinner table when he told that story; I was holding her socked foot to my mouth, kissing it again and again while she ate, while she reached for my glasses and my hair and my necklace. I was trying not to cry with my father. I was trying to be that girl who fell in love with Chris and wanted to marry her because she believed everything she once dreamed of was still hers to have, and to hold.

11 | The Church on the Hill

When Grace was five weeks old, Steve baptized her at his church, a two-hundred-year-old Congregational church on a hill. Chris had found the church, which was called West Cummington Congregational, or West Cummington for short, when she joined a peace and justice study group led by Steve. After a few meetings of the study group, Chris asked me if I wanted to go to the Sunday morning service with her. This was an unexpected reversal: she had never wanted to go to church before now. But she was drawn to the unorthodoxy of the place and of Steve, who was also a sheep farmer and a poet. I went with her a few times after I stopped going to Mass, and I liked it, despite the fact that Steve hardly ever mentioned Jesus. A few months before Grace was born, Chris wanted us to become members of West Cummington. Part of me was excited for the chance to start over in a new church. But mostly I was reluctant.

I met with Steve one June afternoon to discuss joining West Cummington. "I'm actually Catholic," I said, "which is tricky right now." I smiled and looked down at my enormous stomach. I had become my own perfect excuse for my avoidance of the Church—a pregnant woman married to another woman— although I could see that Steve wasn't totally convinced.

"I'd love to know," he said, "genuinely, since it's not my tradition, what you find there."

"Well," I said, not knowing how far to go, how much to say, "I love communion."

"Transubstantiation." He said the word with a certain gusto that, while not disrespectful, was also not entirely reverent.

"Yes," I said, wondering what he would think of me if I told him I believed in it. But Steve was so kind, and even though I didn't know him well, I was certain that he had heard much more complicated stories than a pregnant woman's magical beliefs.

"You know," I said with a shrug, "it's this way for me to have a sort of love affair with Jesus." Oh my God, did I really say that? My cheeks burned with embarrassment. I looked down at the floor.

Steve leaned back in his chair, nodding vigorously. "Now that," he said, "is something I can understand."

I didn't know many people at West Cummington, although they all seemed to know each other extremely well. This was my experience everywhere I went in this small town where we lived now, all these shoulder-to-shoulder circles with no space for anyone new. And even the people who welcomed me at church had little interest in socializing. I was beginning to understand that people who lived in the hills were there because they valued their privacy and independence. The families I was getting to know were kind, but they were islands.

The church itself was a white clapboard building with tall paned windows and a bell tower. Inside there was only the sanctuary and a small entryway, no fellowship hall, no running water. There was a scattering of apple trees in the churchyard and a steep and rocky hillside so close to the back of the church that when you pushed open the swollen wood door behind the last pew you were met with only green and soil and ledge. The room slanted gently so that those in back were afforded a view of the minister in front. There were no adornments—no cross, no stained glass windows, just a grand piano, a wooden pulpit, and red carpeting down two side aisles. As is customary in a Congregational church, there was no center aisle. Chris and I had moved to the land of Congregationalists, of Emerson and Alcott and all their brethren, and it seemed to me that this church would please them all to no end. I wouldn't have minded a center aisle. I wouldn't have minded a little ceremony, a few brushes of gilt. "I would like a little more Jesus," I often said to Chris when, driving home on Sunday mornings, she asked me what I thought of the service. As though I didn't know where to find him.

On the Sunday morning of Grace's baptism, Steve called us to the front of the sanctuary. Before the baptism, all the congregants had dipped their fingers into a bowl of water from the stream that ran below the church, offering their blessings and wishes for Grace. Now Steve took that water in his cupped hand and let it fall through his fingers onto Grace's head. Later my mother would say how pleased she was by the volume of water he used. "I like a good dousing," she said. I nodded my agreement, although in reality I was a little taken aback by all that water.

When Steve baptized Grace, when he asked us all his official questions, questions about our desires for her baptism and our devotion to her growing faith, I was nodding and saying yes, saying we will, but I was thinking of Father Dowling, I was remembering how he had once explained baptism and original sin to me, all those years ago at St. Patrick's. "What if at the moment before baptism," he had said, with that inimitable smile, "the baby in my arms is absolutely perfect? What if it is her world—her new world—that is broken?" He held his arms in a cradle then, moved them slowly back and forth. "What if it is those who came before her who have strayed, doing wrong by each other and by God? Then the water must be to protect her," and with that he dropped an invisible handful of water over the invisible baby in his arms, his fingers opening like a firework. "Baptism seals the perfect and unformed self against the darkness of the world, but also," and he raised his finger to emphasize his point, "baptism acknowledges that the child contains the darkness, not because of anything she has done, but because this is her world now." And with that he folded his hands on his lap and glanced over at the notes he seemed to never follow.

"By what name is this child known?" Steve asked us, jolting me from my daydream, my vision. I answered him with Grace's whole long name, all the other names she might have had long forgotten. He lifted Grace's wet head to his lips and whispered to her, kissed her, and handed her back to Chris.

At home that afternoon I sat on the couch nursing a sleepy Grace while everyone talked and mingled. Again I thought of St. Patrick's. What if we had baptized Grace there? What if I had handed her over to Father Dowling and he had drizzled holy water on her head—that stale water, steeped in marble—and recited the liturgy and above us there were the carved angels and the stained glass, everything glowing, everything the color of sunlight?

12 | Milk Dud

During the first winter of Grace's life I took her into the snowy woods behind our house nearly every day, sometimes on snowshoes, sometimes on skis. I zipped her into a down snowsuit and strapped her to my chest in a Baby Bjorn. She was happy in the cold air; she fell asleep without crying and woke content, two things she did not do inside. On the weekends Chris went out with me, and on clear mornings we pushed Grace in the jogging stroller down the ice-rutted road to the river, where the sounds of water tumbling over ice and rock soothed her into a long sleep. When we came back home, Chris stoked the fire in the woodstove and I nursed Grace in a wooden Adirondack chair I had pulled close to the fire for the winter. We talked while Grace ate, and if I was lucky enough for Grace to doze off for a few minutes, I would lean back and sleep myself, my shirt still open, Grace's lips still attached to my breast.

Most everything Chris and I remembered from the first year of Grace's life was about sleeping, or not sleeping. "What do you remember that was good?" I asked Chris when Grace was much, much older. "Give me a lovely memory."

She thought for a moment. "Remember when we used to light the fire early in the morning when you got up to nurse her and then we would all go back to sleep in front of it?"

"Sort of," I said. "But can you remember anything lovely that happened while she was awake?"

"She was a really beautiful baby," Chris said, "but she cried a lot."

Chris took a four-week maternity leave after Grace's late-summer birth. The leave was unpaid because she had not herself given birth; it was the same leave offered to men at her company. Chris had made the conscious decision to be out as a lesbian at this job, telling her boss at the first interview that she was moving to Massachusetts to live with her girlfriend. Being out made everything different. She kept pictures of the two of us on her desk; I went to office holiday and dinner parties; when I called Chris and her assistant picked up the line, we chatted about grandchildren and gardening. And her colleagues were great sports about both our wedding and pregnancy. They gave us a party a few weeks before we were married, and another before Grace was born, at which they showered us with generous and thoughtful gifts.

All the women Chris worked with who were mothers had either husbands who worked part-time or nannies. In Philadelphia Chris had been one of the guys, but here, as a married lesbian with a baby, she was different than both the working fathers and the working mothers. She had more familial responsibilities than her male counterparts and, I think, more guilt. But not as many responsibilities or as much guilt as the women she worked with. Because she had what they didn't: a wife, who was at home with her baby.

When Grace was a few weeks old we took her to Chris's office, and the women all wanted to talk with me, wanted to hear about the birth and to reminisce about postpartum hormones and pumping breast milk at their desks and a six-week maternity leave that had turned into a year, had turned into two years. The men all wanted to hold Grace. They fought with each other for the chance to lift her up in the air, to lay her across their laps. The company's general counsel, whose children were all in high school now, assured Chris and me that the colicky babies were the smart

Milk Dud

ones, the ones who didn't sleep well were the smartest of them all. He was a kind man, gray-haired and tall. He held Grace in one hand, his arm along her back, his palm a cradle for her head.

I didn't have colleagues for whom I could proudly unwrap Grace and introduce her by name, no one to whom I could show off her curly blonde hair and elfin smile. I had finished my MFA the summer before Grace was born, and in the weeks that followed graduation my school friends had moved away for fellowships and teaching positions. Even my thesis advisor had retired to Manhattan. I had ended one life—the life of the teaching grad student—just before I began my life as a mother. I can see now that this was part of the troubles that were slowly rising in me: it's a risky proposition to become a mother at a time when you aren't also something else.

Before Grace was born we thought we might do some traveling during Chris's maternity leave. Maybe the beach for a little while, or New York. After all, who knew when Chris would have so much time off from work again? But Grace cried too much and slept too erratically for us to travel with her. Soothing her each evening took hours of Herculean effort: walking, bouncing on a yoga ball, doing deep knee bends with her swaddled and pressed against our chests. Chris made CDs of the songs that seemed to quiet her, songs by Joni Mitchell, Ritchie Havens, Cat Stevens. She was our seventies baby. Chris burned the CDs on our computer and then made up titles for them, labeling each disk with a Sharpie: "Milk Dud," "Blast Off Waltz," "Morning Bliss." Eventually we discovered that k.d. lang's cover of "A Case of You" could soothe Grace like no other song could, and so Chris made a CD that was a continuous loop of it. When we put the CD on in the car, Grace would almost immediately stop crying and start looking out the window pensively, as though remembering many a lonesome evening spent in the blue TV screen light. Chris and I couldn't stop laughing the first time we put on the song and saw Grace's wistful expression. "I feel like we should offer her a sippy cup of scotch," Chris said.

Grace was a fast baby. She was born after five hours of labor and twenty minutes of pushing. She could finish nursing in less than ten minutes (both sides) and finish a nap in twenty-five. And until she was a year old, she only napped in our arms, or in her stroller, never in her crib or in the white wicker Moses basket my mother had kindly bought for me a few weeks before Grace was born. Grace took approximately one nap in that Moses basket, a nap my mother clocked at thirteen minutes long. By the time Grace was two weeks old the Moses basket was entirely filled with diapers and burp clothes and pacifiers still in their wrapping. I kept it only because I thought maybe someday Grace would want it for her dolls, a thought that I now admire for its perspective and its hope, considering how little of either I had in those days.

For months we tried to get Grace to sleep without us, letting her cry for ten then fifteen then twenty minutes, letting her cry until even Ferber himself would have picked her up. Grace was a beautiful baby, but she cried a lot.

And so she slept on us, because we needed the peace and quiet when and how we could get it. I often slept while I held her, or occupied myself by picking the cradle cap out of her hair, rubbing away the rivers of lint that gathered in the deep creases of her palms. I also read the *New Yorker*, mostly because its columned pages required only infrequent turning. But Chris read books while she held Grace. That first year she read Tolstoy and Dickens, historical biographies and political commentaries. And in the beginning, when the colic was at its worst and we would split the particularly bad afternoons into thirty-minute shifts, Chris spent her thirty minutes off in the attic drinking beer and reading the *9/11 Commission Report*, while I spent mine reading Dr. Sears and watching the *Happiest Baby on the Block* video. I saw Grace's crying as something to fix; Chris saw it as something to escape.

Our different experiences of Grace's colic were born of many things, but none of them as formative as our vastly different hormone levels, and the way mine turned me, always and entirely, toward Grace. It took me a long time to understand that Grace's crying didn't sound the same to Chris as it did to me. Yes, it was exhausting and agitating, and yes, she wanted it to go away, but the basic—and maddeningly complicated—difference was that it did not fill her breasts with milk, milk that would either be accepted as succor or—more often than not—rejected and left to swell and leak.

Which brings us, as something surely must, to the new differences between Chris's and my body. When we were leaving the hospital the day after Grace's birth, we passed a woman who was getting a tour of the birthing center. "You look amazing!" the woman said to Chris, who was carrying Grace in her infant car seat. "Thanks," Chris said, "but I didn't give birth, my wife did." The woman looked at me then, in my blue velour yoga pants and flip flops, and she was clearly worried. At the time I thought her concern was funny. I had given birth less than twenty-four hours before and I felt like a rock star, like a goddess. I felt bad for anyone who hadn't done what I did, including Chris. But later, when that pride and pleasure faded and I could not believe the state of my body, it was harder to see Chris so unchanged. I watched how she got up from the couch without using her hands, how she ran until sweat streamed down her face and dried on her cheeks. How she drank a beer at five o'clock every afternoon and ate half a block of cheddar cheese for lunch. Because, why not? It was her body after all. It belonged only to her.

We spent Grace's first Christmas with my family in Colorado Springs. My parents lived in an old neighborhood of wide, tree-lined streets, and Chris and I walked them with Grace, marveling at the sun's heat, the sidewalks free of snow. Some afternoons we walked through the campus of Colorado College to the downtown shops and cafés of my childhood. The city where I grew up was relatively large, but my neighborhood was insular, and so when we were out walking we often ran into people I knew. "Looks like you've got news," an old high school friend called out when she saw us walking toward her on the street. Chris was wearing Grace in the Bjorn. Wearing Grace had become like driving, something I never did when Chris and I were together.

"I do," I said, hugging my friend. "This is Chris," I said, putting my hand on Chris's arm, "and this is our baby, Grace."

Chris and my friend shook hands, exchanged greetings. Had my friend known I was married to a woman? If she were surprised, she didn't show it.

"How old is she?" my friend asked.

"Four months," Chris said, leaning down to kiss Grace's head. Kissing Grace's head had become an unconscious gesture for Chris, like brushing hair from her own forehead or turning her watch around her wrist.

"I had her in August," I said quickly. I often went out of my way to tell people that I was the one who had given birth. Surely Chris must have noticed me doing this, but she never said anything about it, never asked me why I felt the need to clarify. She just let me do it.

In early February, Chris went to Germany on business. The morning she left she rose early, put on her long underwear and Carhartts, and went outside to stack wood. When Grace had worked her way through her baby circuit training system (approximately one contented minute in a swing, saucer chair, floor gym, and doorway jumper), we went outside to check on Chris.

Chris loved stacking wood. She loved everything about our woodstove; she didn't even mind going outside in zero-degree weather to dump the ash pail. I also loved the woodstove, or at least I loved the heat it threw, how it warmed our house in a way no radiator ever had. But I didn't like the work of it. I didn't like coming home in the late afternoon to a cold stove, having to leave Grace to cry in her car seat while I got the fire going again. I suspected that Chris loved the tasks of stacking wood and splitting kindling and dumping ashes because they were a way of taking care of Grace without actually holding her. Lately I couldn't see the point in any living situation that involved such labor. I fantasized about co-op living, about having a super, a maintenance man.

"Is this going to be enough?" Chris asked. She had filled both wood holders on the porch. I stood between them, dancing with Grace, who was fussy and slippery in her down snowsuit.

"We'll be fine," I told her. "Although I can't believe you're going. Why do they need you to go?"

"I have to go," she said, not really answering my question. "I can't make that mistake again."

She was referring to an out-of-town hearing she had missed two weeks after Grace was born. She had explained she was on a maternity leave (though she had not been pregnant) and that her baby was too young to leave. But still people had not been happy with her. "A man would've gone," Chris had said when she told me about her boss's cool response to her decision not to go. "And a mother who had given birth would have still been on paid maternity leave," I had pointed out. "Which might have been even worse," she had said. "Who knows?"

So this time there was no question that she would go, although I was still not entirely sure why this meeting couldn't be postponed, or why she couldn't do it over the phone. But I didn't say that. Instead I told her it seemed we had more than enough wood for the week, and would she mind taking Grace for a little while, so I could also get a few things done?

I didn't want Chris to go to Germany, and yet I knew I could manage. And it wasn't as though Chris wanted to go, which made my protests more unreasonable. Lately it seemed she liked her job less, and that she worried about work and money more. Grace was only six months old but Chris often talked about college and how we would pay for it, about the cost of insurance premiums and how many good earning years she had before retirement. She talked about how she was already looking forward to retirement. When we were in Colorado and out for brunch (our first date since Grace was born), Chris told me she had sent away for an application to the Kennedy School of Government.

"Really?" I asked, with perhaps a bit too much surprise in my voice.

"I've always wanted to go back to school," she said. "I've been a lawyer for a long time."

She had been a lawyer for twelve years, which didn't seem like a long time to me, but since I had never had the same job for more than three years I was in no position to question.

"I'm thinking of applying next year," she said. "They have family housing."

I saw the three of us in some cold and teeny one-bedroom apartment in Cambridge, Grace and I in the basement doing laundry while Chris was in class.

My face must have betrayed something of my horror at the image, because Chris said, "You think it's a bad idea."

It is a bad idea! I wanted to say. But I didn't. "No, no I don't," I said. "I'm just not sure about the timing."

"I'm not getting any younger."

This was another thing Chris was always saying now that we had a baby. She wasn't getting any younger. "You're only thirty-seven," I would say. Although secretly I thought thirty-seven sounded really, really old.

When we got back to my parents' house and Chris went upstairs to take a nap, I told my mother about Chris's plan. "She wants to go to graduate school! At Harvard!" I shrieked. Grace, who was nursing, popped off my nipple and looked up at me with alarm. I smiled at her with a don't-you-worry-everything's-fine smile, and gently pushed her back on.

My mother laughed. "When you were two months old your father felt compelled to get his scuba certification. So every Tuesday night he went to the high school pool for scuba training, then he got certified at a flooded quarry."

I vaguely remembered this story, remembered taking my father's flippers and scuba mask with its tempered glass lens on our California beach vacations.

"It's what they do," my mother said. "It's a lot of pressure, providing for a child, for a family. She sees a long road ahead of her. Don't get in her way; let this run its course."

I felt better after talking with my mother, but I wasn't entirely certain that Chris's professional restlessness and my father's scuba dream were the same. I wanted them to be, wanted Chris to devote herself to something rewarding, something that would help her to feel free and young and independent, all while still keeping her job.

While Chris was away, Kelly and Gaby invited me over for dinner. Kelly was a fantastic cook—she moved in the kitchen with the same brisk confidence with which she had run the Sisters Inc. board meetings. Because Gaby was always on kid duty (their son, Emmet, was a toddler) when Kelly was making dinner, she could devote herself to cooking the delicious versions of the comfort foods of her southern childhood. Tonight it was pork roast with apples, which she served on a table set with perfectly mismatched antique china plates.

"I just don't know how she can be away from Grace!" Kelly said as she cut the pork roast into small pieces, quickly blowing on one and then another, putting them in front of Emmet. Whatever Kelly's philosophical objections to motherhood had been, she appeared to have traded them for a close adherence to her and Gaby's fully equitable parenting arrangement. Fifty-fifty everything was their motto. Kelly did half the weekday childcare and half the bedtimes, half the gruesomely early mornings of hot cocoa and two episodes of Miffy. She was vigilant in her care of Emmet, and often critical of what she saw as Chris's less engaged nonbiological parenting. She often referred to Chris as Dad, which, obviously, she did not mean as a compliment.

"She had to go," I said. "It's her job."

It was late when Chris returned home from Germany. There had been a storm and her plane was delayed; the roads home from the airport had been icy and slow. She was tired, and so was I. But unfortunately Grace was not. So I made Chris some scrambled eggs, which she ate standing up, with Grace in her arms. The trip was good, she said; she was glad to have gone. "But it was so hard to be away from you," she said. And I knew she meant Grace, or that she meant the me that was Grace's mother, not necessarily the me that was her wife. She told me that there had been one night when she hadn't been able to reach me, and, not wanting to keep calling and risk waking Grace, had lain awake until dawn, in her quiet luxury hotel, worrying.

We went into the living room and Chris unpacked the gifts she had brought back: some small wooden toys, a soft pink sweater with flower buttons, a picture book in German about the Alps. I would like to tell you what Chris brought me but both of us have tried and tried to remember and we can't. "I remember how late we slept the next morning," Chris said when I asked her about the gift. Again with the sleep. But honestly that was what I remembered too, sleeping away the first full morning of her return. I was exhausted from a week of only half-sleeping until Grace's first night-waking. Usually Chris brought her to me then, and often I didn't even hear her cry, but because Chris was away I had to get up from the warm bed and fetch her myself, and the anticipation of her waking kept me up. Then while she fed I lay awake, wondering how the rest of the night would go, worrying about how tired I would be in the morning.

When Grace woke on that first night Chris was back, Chris didn't hear her and so I jumped up and got her myself—more out of a newly formed habit than consideration. I brought her into the bed with us, tucked her in beside my bare breast and listened to the two of them—Chris nearly silent in her jet-lagged sleep, Grace and her rhythmic sucking, and I could bear my wakefulness and I could bear the thought of morning; I could feel my breathing and my blood slow, I could feel sleep roll over me like a nearly holy fog.

Florida | 13

In the years between my Catholic confirmation and Grace's birth, my church attendance grew increasingly sporadic, but I never missed a Holy Thursday service. It was my favorite night of the liturgical year, and had been since that first Holy Thursday when I woke up with Chris in my apartment and a gold cross around my neck. That night I went down the block to St. Patrick's in the rain, walked up the slick stone steps, pulled open a carved wooden door, and entered the brightly lit nave.

I didn't know what to expect but took my seat and read the unfamiliar prayers, enjoying their novelty. Before the Mass was performed, before the long and—even to me—overly dramatic priestly procession of the Eucharist, I watched Father Dowling bend on one knee to wash the bare and bright feet of three nuns. The nuns, old and sweet-faced and a bit stooped, were dressed in full habits. In turn they leaned down to pull off their black shoes and black socks and lower their feet into the metal basin. When Father Dowling finished washing the last woman's feet, she put her hand on his shoulder and he reached up to hold it.

That night, after the service, Chris had met me on the stairs of St. Patrick's, her gym bag slung over her shoulder. I stopped on the stair above her, laughing as I bent down to kiss her cheek. She laughed too, but took me by the hand and led me down the stairs. "I don't kiss girls who are taller than I am," she said. We went to dinner then, at a dark café around the corner from the church, and I remember we sat next to an open window; I remember there was a small, square planter of grass on the table. I remember that I believed, for the entirety of that dinner, in the possibility of my impossible life.

In the years that followed I looked forward to Holy Thursday even when I was trying to keep my distance from everything else about the Church. Holy Thursday was irresistible. It was that row of nuns' feet, that man kneeling with his basin of water. It was the Last Supper in all its drama: anxious disciples in an occupied city, a beloved and tired Jesus, that holy and human swirl of love and betrayal and good-bye. And then, the last hours of his body and his voice. What could be more thrilling?

But the year that Grace was born I forgot all about Holy Thursday until nearly midnight when I was standing at the bathroom counter decanting shampoo into travel-sized bottles, preparing for an early morning flight to Florida. My heart sank when I remembered the day. I could have washed Grace's feet! How lovely that would have been, how sad to think I had missed a chance to make a simple offering, an acknowledgment. But an offering to whom? To God or to the self I was supposed to become? And what exactly did I want to acknowledge? That I still cared about the Last Supper? That I still felt Jesus near me, felt his quiet and loving companionship? I did not. And this is what I couldn't admit then: I did not miss him. And this absence of desire—never mind his actual absence—made me feel like a failure.

So I had turned my face to another sun, which despite all the work and worry gave me extraordinary pleasure. And while I was not a perfect mother to Grace and these were far from perfect months, she was clearly the miracle I was getting right.

Grace and I were flying to Florida to see my nana, who was eighty-five years old when Grace was born. Nana had a stroke a few weeks before we were scheduled to arrive. It was a small stroke; she suffered no lasting impairments. My mother had heard she was recovering well, but when we got to Nana's house she didn't greet us at the door. She called out a tired hello to us from the living room, where she was resting in her recliner. My mother, who had flown in from Colorado and met me at the airport, looked at me. We both knew this was not a good sign. Perhaps the stroke was not so little after all. We leaned down to give Nana long hugs and kiss her soft skin, brown and freckled from twenty-five years in the Florida sun. She cried when we hugged her, which she had never done before.

Nana's face had changed since I last saw her. At first I thought it was only the passage of time, but that wasn't really it. It was more of an emptying. "It's so good to see you, Nana!" I said, over and over. "So good to be here." I wanted to put my head in her lap, wanted to feel her long fingers in my hair, the cool metal of her rings against my forehead and cheeks. But Grace was in her lap now, her head between Nana's freckled hands.

After a few minutes Grace began to squirm, so I scooped her up and sat her on the floor in front of Nana's chair, I gave her a pile of blocks to knock down and Nana clapped for her. We ate a small dinner together on the sunporch and I fed Grace a few teaspoons of pureed squash from a jar, then read her *My First Book of Sushi.* My mother and Nana finished eating, both of them laughing at how I knew the cardboard pages with their absurd rhymes by heart. I was glad for the chance to make Nana laugh.

Nana gave the three of us her bedroom so that there would be enough space for Grace's Pack 'n Play. I was too embarrassed to tell her that while the extra floor space would be helpful, Grace wouldn't be sleeping in the Pack 'n Play for more than an hour or two. It was Nana's California king bed that we needed, to accommodate our three-generation co-sleeping. As I snapped Grace into her pajamas and curled up on the bed to nurse her to sleep, I remembered a time when I was seven years old and sitting on that very bed in my swimming suit (we were always in our swimming suits in Florida), while Nana showed my mother her new shoes. She pulled the boxes down from a shelf from which later—when I was grown and Nana wore only white Mary Jane sneakers with mesh toes—I would pull shoeboxes full of old birthday cards for us to read. But when I was seven the shoeboxes were too high for me to reach and Nana had no trouble getting them herself. When I was seven the shoeboxes were filled with spectator pumps and a pair of pale-yellow heels with a thin ankle strap. I loved those shoes and knew that someday such things would be mine. I had already shifted my gaze away from my mother with her long, brown hair, her flared jeans and cork sandals. I had already set my sights on Nana in her high heels and coral lipstick, gold chains clasped around her tan neck.

⌀

Several years before our Easter visit, when I was still living in Philadelphia and had just started dating Chris, I flew to Florida for the weekend. The trip was a last-minute one: on Tuesday I woke with a longing for Nana and early Thursday morning I boarded a plane. Nana was still driving then and she greeted me outside the baggage claim with open arms, her eyes shielded by enormous black sunglasses.

When we arrived at Nana's house, she poured iced tea for both of us in cut crystal glasses and motioned me into the living room. "So then," she said, "tell me something."

I knew by this she meant tell me something true, tell me something real. Any topic was fine with Nana so long as it involved love, personal epiphany, or a childhood friend joining the priesthood. So I told her about St. Patrick's, and how I had been going to Mass, that I had joined the confirmation class. I told her that I was happy but also nervous, worried that I would be asked to give up more than I want to. Nana converted to Catholicism before she married my grandfather, so I thought she might have some idea of what I was talking about. I didn't tell her about Hector, or Chris.

"It's about giving over," she said, "that's true." She was smiling, her voice warm. "And there are things you have to give up, there is"—she paused here, picked up her reading glasses from the table next to her, and tapped them gently down again—"renunciation." She smiled at me. "But it was what I wanted." For Nana the Church was about other people: a husband and children, a family life ordered by shared practice and observance. I often thought of Nana in those first weeks and months of visiting St. Patrick's when I watched women herd their children into the pews, women not much older than me, and I wondered if maybe I would also do that someday. But those were fantasies I was trying hard not to entertain. The whole point of St. Patrick's was that it was mine and mine alone. The whole point was that I needed to do what I had never done, which was to sit still and surrender my fantasies and plans.

Later I would think about what Nana said, and the word she used: renunciation. I would realize that perhaps I was selling her short in thinking she didn't have her own personal struggles with what God and the Church asked of her. I could only see then that the Church had not taken from her what I feared it would take from me.

Nana rocked herself up and out of her recliner. She clapped her hands. "Let's go to the beach."

We spent much of the next two days swimming together at the quiet beach near Nana's house. In the late afternoons we rested on her sunporch, then went out for an early dinner in restaurants with views of shallow harbors, their docks lined with rows of clean, white boats. We went to the movies; we looked at old picture albums. We talked about the assisted living she visited a few months ago with my uncle when she was on a trip up north. "Hibernian Hall," Nana said in a dramatic voice. "We were there for afternoon tea, which they served in Styrofoam cups." She laughed. "I hate drinking tea in Styrofoam cups." I swore to Nana that I would rescue her from Hibernian Hall, should she ever find herself there. "I'll take you at your word," she said, still laughing, and put her hand over mine. Then she told me a story. While visiting another of her sons during that same trip, she spent the afternoon with her daughter-in-law's mother, a woman significantly older than Nana. "After lunch," Nana said, "she told everyone that they could bring her home, she was ready to go, but I knew she wasn't ready, not really. I knew she wanted to stay, but she didn't want to be in the way." Nana looked at me, more serious now. "When I say that, when I say you can take me home, don't believe me."

On Saturday afternoon we went to Mass. I sat close to Nana on the slippery wooden pew. I knelt and stood and sat with her; I waited in the pew when she joined the line for communion. She retreated from me during that hour. There were no whispered comments or explanations, no gestures other than a long embrace during the passing of the peace. We left the sanctuary in silence. She paused at the back door to dip her fingers in the stoup of holy water and cross herself, and for a moment I wondered if she would dip her fingers again and cross my forehead, the way she always had when I was young. But she kept walking out of the church and into the still air. "Well, that was lovely," she said, putting on her sunglasses, and then, without waiting for me to comment, took my hand. "I feel like getting a new lipstick," she said. "You?"

When Nana and I hugged good-bye at the airport the next morning I couldn't keep myself from crying. We were standing at the terminal drop-off, the sun already bright on our faces. Nana let go of my shoulders and took my hands in both of hers. I felt the familiar smooth surface of her thick wedding band on my palm. I wanted to say something, to explain the crying, but Nana spoke first. "Rosebud," she said (she had called me Rosebud all through my childhood, although she hardly ever did now that I was grown), "you go home and find the good parts. There are so many good parts. Leave the hard things here with me. I can take care of them for you." She shrugged as if to say my burdens would be no trouble for her. "You can think of me here and how much I love you. You can remember that it doesn't have to be so hard." She squeezed my hands, then let them go to smooth my hair, to touch my cheeks.

I arrived home and called Chris at her office. She was an ambitious associate in a large law firm: she was at her office all the time, even on warm Sunday afternoons. As I waited for her to pick up the phone, I knew that I would ask her if she wanted to have dinner, and I knew she would say yes.

On Monday afternoon I was in Hector's office, telling him what Nana had said. "She said it doesn't have to be so hard," I told Hector. This is what I didn't say: there is a different way to do this. There is a way to want God and also want, in the same breath, affection and companionship. I didn't say these things because if I did I would not be able to hide that I was in love. I didn't say these things because I knew Hector would not, on principle, disagree, but would still tell me that right now it is not possible for me to have both. I didn't say these things because I was not certain he was wrong.

"Maybe she means you don't have to resist the process. You don't have to continually engage in a battle of wills. You can surrender to a will that is not your own."

I deflated. "Maybe," I said. "Maybe she does."

Four years after that visit I wrote to Nana to tell her I was getting married, and that I was marrying a woman. I told her that I hoped she would know I was still the same granddaughter I had always been. A few days after I sent the note, I came home to a message from Nana on the answering machine telling me, in a voice broken with emotion, that she was happy for me and loved me dearly, and that would never change. And two days later I received a letter in which she apologized for that emotion in her voice, and assured me that she was not sad but only worried that I thought marrying Chris would change the way she felt about me. "My love for you is everlasting," she wrote.

The week before our wedding a box arrived addressed to me in Nana's beautiful script. Inside was a set of six Limoges dessert plates that had belonged to Nana's own grandmother. They were rimmed in gold foil and painted with winding pink rosebuds.

～✖～

On Easter morning Nana decided she would rather eat dinner at home than at the restaurant where she made reservations weeks ago. "I'll go to the store," my mother said while we were getting dressed in Nana's room. "Why don't you stay home with Nana? Her Eucharistic minister is coming over in a few minutes."

I knelt down on the floor next to Grace and restacked her jingling foam blocks. I didn't look at my mother. "Oh, that's okay," I said. "I'm happy to help you with the shopping." I couldn't tell my mother that I hadn't received the Eucharist since I was pregnant with Grace, and that it no longer felt possible. I wish I could have seen then that communion was impossible for hopeful reasons, that I couldn't receive because it still meant so much to me. I had faith! It was a simple fact about me, like my thick hair and bad eyesight. The trouble was I had tried to grow my faith like an annual plant in the garden, tending its showy blooms that had no chance of making it through the winter when I should have been trying for something a little hardier. I should have been trying for roots.

I remembered a phone conversation Nana and I had many Easters ago. "I'm not having a good Easter," I told her. "I don't think it's my holiday. I might not even celebrate it anymore." "Oh sure," she said. "Why not?" ("Why not?" is something we liked to say to each other in what we called our Mary Tyler Moore Days, those years in my early twenties and her late seventies when we were both living alone, figuring out how to pay the bills and make baked potatoes in the toaster oven.) "You can choose your holidays," she said. "But you know, if it's really Easter, then it can't be anything but good."

But it can. Look at us now, Nana, I thought as my mother pulled out of the driveway with me next to her and Grace fussing in the back seat. You are waning and I am turning away. How exactly, I wanted to ask Nana, do I love both you and this baby? And how in the world do I also love God? I used to hope that having a baby would increase my capacity for compassion, my understanding of the mysteries of love. And Grace had done just that. The only problem was, she alone filled my new capacity. I might have had more to give, but I gave it all to her. I was a distant wife, a self-absorbed daughter, and an absent friend. And I could live with all that. Or I should say I did live with that, in the same way I lived with my dizzying and unwieldy love for Grace. But I was maxed out. I knew that I could not bear the fragile beauty of Nana and Jesus on the sunporch. Would I ever be able to stop crying?

As I write this I think of how lovely it would have been to stay home with Nana that Easter morning, although I have long since forgiven myself for choosing instead to push Grace around Publix in a shopping cart. In the years since that Easter morning I have often imagined that I made the other choice, and in my mind's eye I can see myself sitting next to a weakened Nana; I can feel Grace on my lap. I can see myself crying and crying, but I can also see the moment when I stop. This imagining is a sort of prayer, really, and when I pray it I am reminded of something Andre Dubus wrote, about how he believed that prayer was not beholden to time, and so it was possible to pray for people and events of the past, and for those prayers to ease the way of those long gone. Dubus wrote that he sometimes still prayed for Jack Kennedy. I know my prayer is not the same, I know there is no moment on the sunporch to revisit and nothing can change that, but I still pray for both of us then. And I ask God to ease Nana's loneliness, and my fear.

We went back to the house with a turkey breast and sweet potatoes for roasting, a bunch of thick asparagus stalks, and a box of butter cookies. My mother made dinner and we ate together on the sunporch. Everything was just how Nana liked it and she said so, which, I could see, pleased my mother. After dinner Nana took a nap in her recliner while my mother cleaned up and I entertained Grace.

The next morning we packed our things. "What should I do with this?" I asked my mother, pointing to the travel high chair we bought for Grace at Target. "Maybe I'll put it in the Love Shack," she said, using Nana's moniker for the shed where she kept her washer and dryer and her three-wheel bicycle. I finished packing while my mother talked with Nana. Nana didn't want her to leave. My mother promised that she would come back right away, as soon as she took care of a few things at home. And she would make good on that promise; she would return to Florida in two weeks, and four weeks later Nana would be living in a convent-turned-assisted-living in Pennsylvania, a few miles down the road from Hibernian Hall. I would not be called to rescue her; Nana would enjoy many good years in assisted living. But the other promise, the one about not believing her when she says she wants to go home, I broke that one. Because what Nana was really asking then was for me to conspire with her against the solitude of old age, against the expectation that she would want to fade politely into the background. But that Easter I began to let her fade.

We took the suitcases to the car. Nana sat in her recliner, her back to the door. I went in to say good-bye. I put Grace on Nana's lap one more time and told her I loved her. She kissed Grace, cradled her small head. I took Grace to the car, and a few moments later my mother came out of the house. She got into the driver's seat and backed the car out of the driveway. Just before we made the turn onto the street, Nana came to the door. She waved and blew us a kiss. "Oh, good for her," my mother said. "Good for her for saying good-bye." And Nana stood there at the door, waving, until we turned the corner and she disappeared from view.

14 | Family Week

Provincetown, the fishing village at Cape Cod's easternmost tip, is a shifting land. Water swallows marsh and harbor and then recedes; the sky is the color of melancholy and then optimism, and then a color you simply can't name, which is why the painters love it there. Provincetown is also the land of queer tourists and our festivals, our weeks. In summer there is Carnival, in fall Spooky Bear Weekend and Women's Week. And in winter, Snowbound Leather. When Grace was two years old we took her to Family Week. It was Gaby and Kelly's idea: they had a favorite rental in the quiet East End, a butter-yellow Victorian with tumbles of wisteria over the gate and trompe l'oeil doors. We made the plans in early February, when the arrival of summer had seemed as improbable as Grace sleeping through the night. But now we were here. (Although Grace was still not sleeping through the night.)

I loved Provincetown. Chris preferred the wildness of Truro, the quiet of Wellfleet, but I loved the people in Provincetown; I loved the harbor and the gleaming library, the dress shops, the beautiful, beautiful men. It was in Provincetown, many years before, that a gay man had explained his theory of why gay men weren't always so kind to lesbians. The man, a charming and talkative psychologist from Atlanta, was a fellow guest at the inn where Chris and I were spending New Year's, and where we were one of only two lesbian couples. (Chris had a crush on one of the women. She kept saying, "Doesn't Helen look just like Christiane Amanpour?")

"Gay men admire the feminine, and lesbians reject it," the psychologist from Atlanta explained to me over breakfast. "They have what we want, and don't do much with it." Then he winked at me and said, "A rule to which you are an exception."

I laughed and thanked him, delighted that this stranger could see exactly who I was. Of course, I was really delighted because he could see exactly who I *wanted* to be: a lesbian who didn't look like a lesbian. I had very little understanding then of femme culture and identity, and that I was not an exception but a type. I knew about femmes, but I thought of them only in the past tense, as highly costumed women on the arms of stone butches in lesbian bars. I could only see them in black and white. Where I lived, most of the lesbians—really most of the women in general—fell somewhere between femme and butch, right around Teva sandals and Title Nine running shorts. And because these were the first days of the new millennium and the internet was still in its infancy, I didn't have the chance to view—daily, hourly—a varied and multitudinous array of lesbian lives. I couldn't have imagined doing what I now do several times a day: scrolling through the Instagram feeds of lesbian writers and ministers, politicians and journalists, artists and designers. I look at their glasses and their girlfriends, their tote bags and cocktails, their book piles and vacation photos. Their Easter dresses.

But these women and their worlds weren't visible to me in those days. All I had were my outdated assumptions, and my fierce refusal to admit that my sexual identity had a lot more to do with my monogamous three-year-long relationship with a woman than it did with how many pairs of shoes I owned.

During Family Week all the gay men were fathers. At restaurants, at the playground and the beach, I saw them with their babies and toddlers and kids. I saw them talking on cell phones, I saw them flirting with each other, and I even saw them chatting with the lesbian moms. I saw them looking really, really good. I admired their ability to parent and remain self-centered.

"That's sort of homophobic," Kelly pointed out when I told her I had far lower parenting expectations for gay men than I did for just about anyone else. And then, before I could defend myself, she laughed and said, "But so do I."

Her laughter emboldened me. "I also think they're having more sex than we are," I said.

"You think?" she said, rolling her eyes.

Provincetown was a refuge, a wonderland for so many gay people, and when we were there I was reminded that the ease with which we lived in western Massachusetts was a luxury. All these other LGBT parents came to Provincetown for the chance to be themselves, to rest in the glorious gayness of the place. But I didn't need that rest in the same way. Not that I surrounded myself with queer people. Quite the opposite, really. Even though we lived in the lesbian capital of America, most of my friends—aside from Gaby and Kelly—were straight. My straight friend Heather was always telling me about a lesbian she had just met, how I should become friends with her. "You need some lesbian friends," she would say. I knew she was right, but I was happy with the friends I already had. They were more familiar to me than the lesbians I knew.

I thought of Allie, my "little sister" from Sisters Inc., many times during Family Week. I thought of how many of the women and men around me had asked themselves the same questions Chris and I had, and how they had come to a different conclusion about how best to become a parent, and I was awed by them and their children, everyone's bravery, everyone's faith.

On our first morning in Provincetown, we took the kids to Race Point for some real waves. While Chris and Gaby tried to show them how to stay on their boogie boards, Kelly and I read on the beach. Kelly was reading *Confessions of the Other Mother*, a collection of essays written by nonbiological lesbian moms. When I asked her how it was, she made a face and said, "Not great, really. But I want Chris to read it. I'm curious what she thinks."

I didn't tell her that there was no way in hell Chris was going to read that book. Chris—unlike Kelly and me—did not seek out motherhood narratives. She was wise in this regard: as both Kelly and I could attest, it was nearly impossible to find an account of motherhood—lesbian or straight—that resonated. I had already skimmed *Confessions of the Other Mother*, and I knew Kelly didn't like it because none of the essays told her story.

The four of us moved in rotation during our week in Province-town: two mothers on duty, two mothers off, which meant that I didn't see much of Chris. Instead I stood in the waist-deep water at Herring Cove with Gaby, hoisting the children onto their plastic floating alligators, laughing as we watched the dads march their complaining children all the way down the beach to the gay end of the cove. "Why can't we stay here?" we heard kid after kid ask, dragging their beach bags through the sand, gesturing to an open spot next to a two-mom family. Their fathers ignored them and kept walking. "I'm with the kids," Gaby said. "Why not stay here? Same water."

"You can't give up everything," I said.

Gaby squinted at me, said nothing.

"Okay, you can," I said. "But isn't it kind of great that they aren't?"

Grace refused to take a nap in her rented crib—the afternoons were hot and she was too excited by the idea of her playmate Emmet right downstairs. And so Chris, despite the heat and lack of shade, pushed Grace around town in the stroller until she fell asleep. Gaby stroller-napped Emmet too, and while they were both out, Kelly and I sat in the house's cool kitchen looking at magazines and talking.

"Can I help?" I asked one afternoon, as Kelly was getting ready to cook an early dinner.

"You sit," she said. "You don't ever get to. Cooking is relaxing for me."

I felt the sharp edge of everything Kelly said about what I did and didn't get to do. I read so much into her assessment of me, even more since a conversation a few months before when I had asked about her plans for Mother's Day. "Oh, Gaby and I are too radical for Mother's Day," she had said. "But I can see how it would be important for someone in your situation." I hadn't said anything in reply, but that night when I relayed the conversation to Chris, I burst into tears.

"Which situation, exactly?" Chris asked.

"The one where you go to work and I take care of our kid," I said, wiping my face with the back of my hand. "We're lesbians. We're supposed to deconstruct the patriarchal model, not replicate it."

Chris howled with laughter. "Did Kelly actually use those words?"

I laughed too, a loud and barky half cry, half laugh. "Well, not exactly, but she hinted."

Chris pulled me to her and kissed me hard. I pulled away. "This is exactly what Kelly's talking about." But Chris pulled me in again, and I didn't resist.

"She really pushes your buttons, doesn't she?" Chris said.

"Why doesn't she push yours?" I asked, resting my head on her shoulder.

"Because I don't really care what she thinks of me."

I wanted to say, that's because what she thinks of me is worse. But it was too hard to make Chris understand that there was a hierarchy of mothers, and she was above me in it. She had a child *and* a career. She might be conflicted, she might feel guilty about getting home late, about missing bedtime or music class, but she was conflicted because she was striving and ambitious and engaged. She was conflicted because motherhood was something that had added to her identity, not usurped it.

But I knew Chris would simply dismiss all that. She was adamant about the importance of my life at home with Grace, and while I appreciated that, I didn't appreciate her refusal to acknowledge how complicated our arrangement was. I didn't appreciate the assumptions she made—many of them unconsciously—about the shape and measure of my day, assumptions about what would happen to that egg-crusted cast iron skillet she left on the stove yet found—miraculously clean and dry—back in the cabinet the next morning.

And if I couldn't explain all these things to Chris, then surely I couldn't explain them to Kelly. So when she told me to sit and relax, I did. She sliced shallots and salted fish, carefully removed pith from pink grapefruit and mixed it with chunks of ripe avocado. I put another ice cube in my glass of rosé and flipped open her copy of *O Magazine*. We chatted some, commiserated about preschool admissions and the upcoming season of holidays with our in-laws.

Later, after we had all finished an early dinner and decided to take the children into town for an ice cream, Kelly said she would stay behind. "I need to vacuum," she said.

When Chris and I protested, Gaby told us not to bother. "Kelly loves to vacuum. She's been looking forward to it all day," she explained. We all laughed then—even Kelly—and as we walked to town without her I thought of how lucky it would be to love your work and your chores, to align your desire so perfectly with your responsibilities. It did not occur to me then that perhaps such alignment had less to do with luck than it did intention, with crafting your own resonant and familiar narrative.

One evening when Chris was giving Grace a bath and Gaby was watching *Funny Girl* with Emmet, Kelly and I walked across town to pick up sushi. "Oh, the Martin House," Kelly said wistfully, pointing at the sign for the beloved—and not at all child-friendly— restaurant. "Remember those days?"

I did. Chris and I had last eaten at the Martin House the summer before I conceived Grace. We were vacationing in nearby Wellfleet and I was ovulating. But because we were at the beach, we weren't doing anything about it, a fact I had grieved in the weeks before we left. But my grief, surprisingly, barely made it over the Sagamore Bridge, and by the time we got to Wellfleet it was gone. That week we slept on the second floor of a tiny cottage, in a loft with a view of the water. The cottage's bookshelves were filled with old cooking magazines, *Gourmet* and *Bon Appétit* and *Fine Cooking*, and so each morning I took a stack of them to the beach and learned how to cook. And one night we drove to Provincetown for dinner at the Martin House. I wore a silk dress that tied around my neck and we ate mussels and oysters, drank a bottle of wine. Before dessert I began to feel the familiar twinge in my side, the pressing weight of a swelling ovary. I began to say something to Chris, something clever about a good egg gone to waste, but I stopped myself. If she were a man I might have rushed her through dinner and back to our bed, but she was a woman and we were in no hurry.

I remembered that evening now as my last experience of pure desire for a baby, a desire unblemished by the possibility of failure. That night my treasure, which was not the baby herself but rather my sweet longing for her, returned to me one last time. Three months later, I was pregnant.

"You know," I said to Kelly, "in those days all I wanted was what I have now."

"Wow, that is so sweet," Kelly said. She pulled her sunglasses down onto her face. "But I miss those days like hell."

I missed them too. I missed them like hell. Because in truth I didn't have everything I had wanted then. In trying to conceive—even in pregnancy—I had harbored the illusion that the baby, when she arrived, would slide neatly into the spot my longing for her once filled, peg into hole, and the longing would vanish. But that is not what happened. Grace made her own space; she was both more glorious and more consuming than anything I could have known to want. But the truth was it had been easier to want her. When I wanted her I traveled and worked and loved Chris; I ran steep hills; I read novels and drank wine. I went to bed and woke, and knew nothing of the long hours between, other than my dreams of her. When I longed for Grace I knew exactly who I was. And now she was here—she was two years old!—and I did not know myself. A longing still remained in me, although I could not yet discern its shape, and so I didn't know how to fill it.

In Provincetown we fed the kids early and put them to bed before dark. Gaby and Kelly switched off nights of bedtime, which meant that one of them was always off duty, always ready with wine and cigarettes on the patio. Chris and I did more of a bedtime mash-up: I gave Grace a bath; Chris read to her; I returned to rock her to sleep. Then we spent a good while (especially when on vacation and in an unfamiliar bedroom) going back into her room. I marveled at how Gaby and Kelly could listen to Emmet's crying and not flinch when it wasn't their night. "It's hard," Kelly said to me once, when I asked her about how they split soothing responsibilities, "although not as hard as it was when he was a baby and still nursing. That was torture for me. He only wanted Gaby. Nursing makes co-parenting nearly impossible."

I agreed with her entirely, and yet I would not have sacrificed nursing for a more egalitarian parenting arrangement. Nursing was hard and often painful; it made my range of motion in the world maddeningly small, tethered me to Grace even when she was older and could go hours without my breast. But still I loved it. Those daily—hourly—chances to slake her thirst and quiet her cries were respites from the worry and the stress of decoding her. Nursing slowly weaned me from the miracle of pregnancy to the work of motherhood; it delayed, mercifully, the end of our animal days.

In the evenings, when Emmet and Grace were sleeping, we sat in the falling dark of the yard, ate lobster rolls and take-out sushi, did tequila shots, and lost all track of time. We were not beholden to a babysitter's curfew or tomorrow's morning rush. We didn't even need baby monitors; we just left the bedroom windows open. In Provincetown we had our first conversations in years without the background noise of that terrible, agitating static. Each night we seemed to reach back further, to sink more quickly into stories of our meetings and courtships, old girlfriends (theirs, not mine), our childhoods. Each night I could more clearly see the shape of their scars, their losses. I listened to Chris talk about her family, her many closeted years, and how they both made her work hard, perhaps harder than she needed to, always wanting to prove her worth. Kelly told us that her parents feared her not only because she was gay but because she was smart, and so to move beyond them she made a personal and professional life from her own alchemy of sexuality and politics and intellect. And Gaby, who had been uncomfortable in her female body since she was young, told stories of her transformation into a mannish woman whose body could still conceive the child of her dreams, fulfilling, she believed, the one purpose of her uterus. She talked of how happy she was to be returning to her androgynous self.

And me? I was the girl whose parents—whose entire family—loved her with a deep and even-keeled devotion. My gayness had not cost me a friend, or a colleague. It had not, in the end, even cost me my chance to have a child. Those nights in Provincetown I felt myself cleaved from the three of them; I saw myself as they saw me. As different. "And you," they all said—even Chris, "you wouldn't know."

But I knew. The trouble was, I couldn't explain how. Who would want what I had lost? In the world I lived in no one had God, no one considered herself religious. I knew plenty of observant Jews, but to be Jewish was an entirely different proposition than claiming Christianity. The Jews I knew hung their framed ketubahs over their mantels and their chuppahs over their children's cribs; they mounted mezuzahs in their doorways, gathered with friends to light candles and eat homemade challah on Shabbat. Even the most secular people I knew took no issue with such observances. But Christianity was suspect, and Catholicism was downright absurd.

What I had lost was my sense of entitlement to belief, my place in the world of religion. I thought I could remain faithful in my own small and secret way, but a secret faith can't last. Faith required light, and connections with other believers forged in moments of shared experience, of confessed doubt and wonder. But I did not talk about God with anyone in those days. My friends were not believers, and neither was my wife.

The temperature climbed the whole week we were in Provincetown, and by Thursday it was 90 degrees. Such temperatures were unusual, which was why our butter-yellow Victorian didn't have air conditioning. The rooms were sweltering, and the still afternoon air made being at the beach for more than a few minutes unbearable. One particularly hot afternoon Kelly suggested we take the kids to the pool at the Provincetown Inn. "Tell her there's a bar," she said as I went upstairs to clear the new plan with Chris.

"I didn't come to Provincetown to go to the pool," Chris said. She was lying on the bed in the pizza oven that was our bedroom. Chris was raised spending summers on Cape Cod and she loved nothing more than the ocean; she loved it with the zealous and inflexible love of things past. It was remarkable to me how Chris was able to remain so true to her old desires, her old impulses, despite having a child now. She still wanted what she had always wanted; loved what she had always loved. In many ways I could see—and it worried me—that having a child had returned her to the struggles of her childhood, her lack of agency, of freedom. She hated being accountable to anyone else's schedule; she hated schedules in general. When we were first together, she told me that her sanity is dependent on two things: solitude and exercise. "Exercise," she once said, "is like breathing for me." At the time I was impressed, and I wondered what I needed as much as I needed oxygen. Nothing came to mind. Now that we had a child her fundamentalism annoyed me. "Breathing is the only thing like breathing," I now said when she tried this line on me.

"It's too hot at the ocean," I said.

"Not in the water."

"The kids can't stay in the water for more than a few minutes. It's too cold." This was one of those times when New England in general, and Cape Cod in particular, made no sense to me.

I took off my sundress and pulled on my bathing suit. "Come here," Chris said sleepily, motioning for me.

"We're leaving."

"Just for a second."

I leaned down to quickly kiss her. She pulled gently on the strap of my swimming suit. "I miss you," she whispered.

"I miss you too," I said, although my voice did not match the tone of her whisper, the emotion, and we both knew it. I was rushing; it was true, rushing to get downstairs. I was often rushing then. But I also didn't like it when Chris said she missed me. It made me defensive. She was becoming another person whose

Family Week   127

emotions I was responsible for, who needed something from me that I couldn't quite give.

On our last day in Provincetown there was a Family Week parade down Commercial Street. We tied balloons to Grace's stroller and dressed her in pink Converse sneakers and pink sunglasses. Emmet wore a black tank top with a ♀ on it. Because Emmet and Grace were still young, we hadn't participated in many of the planned Family Week activities: the art and theater workshops, the sand castle competition. Until now I hadn't really experienced the scope of the gathering, its grand and lively energy. We congregated on Commercial Street, which was filled with children. The older ones carried signs decorated with hearts and rainbows; the littles sported costumes: fairy wings and superhero capes, springy bug antennae and crowns. Their faces were painted with rainbows and flowers and soccer balls. Some people sang as we walked; some started chants about love and pride. Most talked loudly and laughed with each other, trying to keep up with their kids, stopping to take pictures and tie shoelaces and lift tired toddlers into wagons and onto shoulders.

The parade ended at the park in the center of town, and the marchers gathered to listen to speeches from Family Week organizers. Gaby and Kelly stood close, arms around each other, looking more affectionate, more comfortable than I had ever seen them. Grace sat on Chris's shoulders. I could tell Chris was a little bored. I listened to the speeches, looked around at the beautiful and buoyant children, and I wondered if Grace would need this parade someday. Would she need to come to Provincetown the first week of August for its consolations of sameness? I loved the sight of the face-painted children, and yet I didn't count Grace as one of them. If someone had asked me why, I would have said, "Oh, we live in western Massachusetts," and I would have smiled and explained, "It's very progressive. We're very lucky." But that was not the reason I didn't see Grace among these children. When that gay man with the southern drawl had leaned over the table on New Year's all those winters ago, he had told me something I still believed about myself: I was the exception. And if I was, then surely so was my daughter.

Eleanor's Desk | 15

To celebrate her fortieth birthday, Chris wanted to climb Mount Washington, the highest peak in the White Mountains of New Hampshire. "Your birthday is in November," I said. We can't climb Mount Washington in November."

"We can. People do it all the time. It's about being prepared."

"To dig a snow cave and freeze to death in it?"

"It's my birthday," Chris said, sounding uncharacteristically childish. "I want to spend it on top of a mountain. Forty is a really big deal. You'll understand someday."

Chris was worked up about turning forty. It seemed that the day had to somehow be everything her life currently was not: independent, adventurous, childless. Romantic. I wanted to be a good wife, to plan something wonderful for her, but I needed her birthday celebration to be something that didn't involve crampons and potential blizzard-condition mountaineering. I thought of suggesting a southern peak, maybe somewhere in the Blue Ridge, but I didn't really want to be that far away from Grace. So instead I suggested other ideas: museums in Manhattan, wine tasting on the North Fork. She didn't like any of my ideas. "What about Rhinebeck?" I asked. "We could go to Val-Kill, to the Roosevelt library." I knew she had wanted to see Eleanor Roosevelt's Hudson Valley home ever since we moved to New England.

"I'll think about it," she said.

Chris didn't want to give up on Mount Washington. I was not sympathetic. We have a two-year-old, I wanted to say. I can't be on a mountaintop in winter with you. I wanted Chris to know this, to understand it as the fact it was, and not to ask me—yet again—if my first loyalty was to her. I did not want to have to say no, actually, it no longer is.

Finally Chris agreed to Rhinebeck, to the Roosevelts. My sister and her boyfriend came to take care of Grace, and early on Friday morning we drove down the rolling and quiet Taconic Parkway into the Hudson Valley. We checked into a tiny inn near the Roosevelt library. Our room was white—white walls, white down comforter and pillows. It had a gas fireplace with a remote control. I turned it on. We took off our clothes and had fast and quiet sex, because we didn't remember how to have the other kind.

The next morning we went to Val-Kill, Eleanor Roosevelt's modest estate. It was early November, and so there were no leaves on the trees but also no snow, which gave the landscape a sense of decay, making the house and grounds seem older and shabbier than they were. We bought tickets for a tour of the house. The tour guide brought us first into Eleanor's dining room, where we stood behind a braided silk cord separating us from the thick-legged oak table set with pale china. The tour guide told us that Eleanor hosted dinners with the best minds of her generation, Nehru, Kennedy, Robert Frost. "Sometimes she would send the cook home and cook dinner herself," the tour guide told us, "despite the fact that the only thing she knew how to cook was scrambled eggs." The tour guide laughed.

I looked at Chris and she shrugged and gave me a look of feigned innocence. Scrambled eggs were also the only thing Chris knew how to cook. At first, when we were dating, I found her culinary ineptitude rather adorable, but lately I found it maddening. And now, listening to the tour guide, I felt like a bit of a fool. If you don't know how to make anything but eggs, you don't make dinner very often. And while I understood that Eleanor didn't know how to make anything other than eggs because she was a woman of privilege, Chris was clearly proof that even women raised in the working class can absolve themselves of all culinary knowledge. After all, both her sisters could cook. But when you don't cook, your thoughts aren't occupied with shopping lists and defrosting times. Your mind is filled with ideas. And your time is filled with work. You eat takeout; you eat the dinner your wife made.

When I was in fourth grade, I did a report on Eleanor Roosevelt. My parents took the time to read my research books with me, to talk with me about Eleanor's descent into the West Virginia coal mines, her invitation to Marion Anderson. I understood even then that Eleanor Roosevelt was the best sort of woman: humble, courageous, and dedicated to justice, and for a long time I strived to be those things, to embody those ideals. But not anymore. Since Grace was born I had become insular and myopic, homebound. I had also become a skilled cook.

After the dining room the tour guide led us into Eleanor's office. The walls were lined with bookshelves, and opposite the hearth was her unassuming desk, its surface covered with neat stacks of papers and books. It was, like the dining room table, staged, but still I felt tears prick my eyes at the sight of it. I looked over at Chris, who was also looking at the desk, but I turned away before I caught her eye. I didn't want to think about Chris then, didn't want to think about what she saw when she looked at the desk. Chris was seven years older than I was, which for a long while made the discrepancies in our professional accomplishments seem reasonable—surely by the time I was as old as she was I would have made comparable career strides. But now she was forty and I was thirty-three, the age she had been when she was offered an in-house counsel job, when the managing partner at the law firm she was leaving came into her office and asked her what he could do to make her stay. And I hadn't even finished my first book. Our discrepancies were no longer a matter of time.

I looked at Eleanor's desk and I saw what I no longer had. My own desk was now covered with Grace's carefully dated crayon scribbles, my to-do lists and Mini Boden return labels. And I only occasionally sat there anyway, to write emails or update a blog I was keeping as a record of Grace's childhood. I hadn't written anything of significance since Grace was born.

After the tour, Chris and I walked slowly through the gardens. The perennials and roses were cut back in anticipation of winter; the shrubs were covered with wooden tipis that would shelter them from the impending snow and ice. Still, the day was warm and we walked without our coats. Chris put her arm around me. "Let's have another baby," she said, "and name her Eleanor."

Another baby! This was the first time Chris had brought up the idea; usually it was me, and usually she said she wasn't sure, wasn't ready. I had hoped for as much from this weekend away, hoped that she would, with a little distance, remember the sweetness of life with a baby and not only the chaos and exhaustion. But I hadn't expected that being away from Grace would make me wonder about a second child. I hadn't expected Eleanor's desk. Still, I couldn't help but take Chris's bait. "You named Grace," I said, leaning into her. "The second one is all mine."

Remodel or Divorce | 16

When I was pregnant with our second child it seemed that all our married friends were either remodeling their kitchens or getting divorced. "Are those the only two options?" Chris asked when I pointed out the trend to her. "I like our kitchen."

"We could do the bathrooms," I suggested.

"Could we go to Italy?"

"No," I said. "That doesn't count."

We were joking, but we were also anxious, Gaby and Kelly were separating. A few weeks before, we had gone out with them for what we suspected would be the last time. They had decided to separate a few days before Kelly's birthday, and while the customary dinner party was off, they still needed to mark the occasion. "For Emmet," Gaby explained when she called to invite us, and I said, yes, yes of course, although I didn't really want to go. But we did, we met for an early dinner on the deck of an old ski lodge that had recently reopened as a restaurant. Chris and Grace and I arrived first, and we rose from the table as the three of them arrived, looking tired and drawn.

"Happy Birthday," I said to Kelly, kissing her cheeks.

"Congratulations, Mama," she said in a tender voice. She gently brushed her hand against my belly, which was already straining my skirt. We gave Kelly a stack of books and a bottle of gin; Gaby gave her some framed artwork of Emmet's. Grace and I left early, offering her bedtime and my nausea as an excuse, and Gaby and Emmet left with us. Chris stayed with Kelly, drank with her by the river for a few hours. We didn't know it then (although I suppose in some ways we did), but Kelly would get us in the divorce. We didn't see Gaby much after that birthday dinner. Sometimes I thought we could have tried harder to remain friends with both of them, but mostly I understood how impossible it would be.

Our second daughter, June, was born in late winter, nearly two weeks after her due date. After such a short, relatively easy labor with Grace, the complications of June's long and painful labor were surprising, and tinged with injustice. She was born in the early hours of the morning, and Chris stayed in the hospital with the baby and me all through that first day and night. My parents were taking care of Grace then, and while I had expected to miss her, to want to get home as quickly as possible, I found I liked the hospital. I liked being alone with June, and with Chris.

Just after dark on that first day, Chris left the hospital and drove the twenty minutes to Northampton for our favorite hamburgers, and we sat together on the hospital bed, eating and talking while June slept in the cradle of my bent legs. Chris told me again and again that she was in awe of what I did to get that baby out; she told everyone she called, everyone who came into the hospital room, how amazing I was. I felt a bit wrecked, honestly, and didn't want to think so much about the birth, although I appreciated Chris's pride, and her recall of details that were entirely hazy to me. All I could remember then was the pain, whose echo still rang in my body. But I was happy. The baby was finally here, and the task of her—which had, three years before, crushed us like a tidal wave—was easy to manage, leaving Chris and me space to pay attention to each other, an attention tinged with the high and relief of birth, with our shared immodesty over the miracle we had wrought.

Remodel or Divorce   135

It was a different story when we returned home. Two children were their own sort of tidal wave. Grace, who adored all things baby and had awaited June's arrival with great anticipation, cried when I scolded her for putting her finger in June's ear. "June is a total bust!" she yelled, then ran to her room and slammed the door as though she had grown into a teenager while we were away.

It was Chris, not me, who offered Grace consolation. During the first weeks of June's life, Chris took Grace on all manner of excursions to places I didn't like and they did: the indoor butterfly pavilion, the pet store, the pizza restaurant that gave children a tiny ball of pizza dough to play with before their dinner arrived. Chris took Grace to the consignment store to buy leotards and let her choose a lavender one made of crushed velvet, which Grace wanted to wear every day. I hated the leotard, and I was annoyed with Chris for buying it. But I didn't say anything. Grace was Chris's responsibility, the way that June was mine. We all missed each other then: I wanted more time with Grace; Chris wanted to hold June while she slept, the way we had held Grace when she was an infant. "Put her down," I would say, in a not-very-nice voice. "This one can sleep without you." I was angry at Chris for what I saw as her elective engagement with June. When she told me she felt as though she didn't even know her, I wanted to reply, "Well, she's free tonight at eleven." But I didn't.

When Grace was a baby, Chris shared the night shift with me, even when she was working again. But she wasn't going to do that now. I could see that much of her involvement the first time around was a result of the great shifting of our lives and our uncertainties about Grace, our anxieties, which we shared. Was she eating enough? Was she warm enough? But it turned out Grace was fine. More than fine, really. So Chris wasn't so vigilant this time. She wasn't worried that June wasn't getting enough food, or that I wasn't drinking enough water. And not only that, Grace had become her responsibility, almost entirely. She drove twenty minutes out of her way each morning to drive Grace to child care so I didn't have to wake June; she bathed and put Grace to bed each night, took her on weekend outings. She answered her calls in the night, even when she called for me, even when upon seeing Chris, she cried, "I meant the other mama!"

But Chris would not get up in the night for June; she would not bring her to me, would not change her diaper before putting her back to sleep. She would not even take an occasional shift with June's 10 p.m. crying jags. And so I spent those nights alone, most often in the bathroom, where June liked the sound of the exhaust fan, liked to look up at the chicken-and-egg mobile I had hung many years ago for Grace, which was now less of a mobile and more just a chicken hanging from the ceiling.

Chris wouldn't take a shift because she had to sleep. "I'm older this time around," she said, "and I've been sleep-deprived for too long. I can't do it again." End of story. Or I should say, end of her story, beginning of mine.

I was starting to see Chris as that imaginary woman we were all told we could be: a woman with children and a career, a woman who knew the importance of exercise and a good night's sleep, who got her hair highlighted every six weeks. It was hard not to see Chris as a rebuke. Of course she could not have had the life she did without me, in the same way I could not have been the person I was, namely a stay-at-home mother—something I had wanted to be—if I didn't have her. But we didn't see each other's lives that way then. We saw each other as obstacles rather than helpmates. We were not really on each other's side. I was frightened by our opposition, by the inky depths I sensed below us when we fought about time and laundry and money, fights during which we both said hurtful things, clenched our teeth with outsized rage. We resolved our fights, sometimes only through a mutual desire to be finished, to stop trying to resolve. I felt us swinging on a weakening rope then, could see us trying to cross a bridge whose splintering boards would hold us, but barely.

During the first two years of Gaby and Kelly's separation, Kelly often slept over at our house. She and Gaby wanted Emmet to remain in his house, which meant that the two of them moved in and out each week. Kelly came into our house like a warm wind, her hair always lovely, her makeup done, her clothes professional and polished. Sometimes Chris would work late and I would put Grace to bed while Kelly tended to June, then after June was asleep we would eat the take-out dinner she brought from town. Sometimes she brought little gifts for Grace, sticker books or bath beads or flip flops, and she read to her before bed, asked her thoughtful questions, told her funny stories. At the time I couldn't understand the breadth of Kelly's loss, how much she missed her own son and how wrenching it might be to spend the evening with someone else's children. It was years before I really understood how hard it had been for her to be away from Emmet. All I could see then was her free time, her leisure.

By the time June was born, Kelly had a girlfriend in New York, so she stayed with us less often, although I still looked forward to the nights when she did. I looked forward to her New York stories. Her new girlfriend was an activist, and a vocal critic of gay marriage. Kelly often shared her regret for buying into an idea and a system that she hadn't even believed in. "There was a critique, but I wasn't listening," she said, berating herself. "But it was also historic, so how could we not? But I was blindsided. So many of us were. But we're not about marriage, you know?"

I didn't answer. I actually was about marriage. Not that I could—or wanted to—defend my allegiance. I was angry with my wife most of the time; I was always tired and often lonely. I wasn't exactly a poster child for personal fulfillment through lifelong commitment.

Remodel or Divorce

June stayed up late and slept in—she would have made a delightful first baby—but I had to get up and make Grace's lunch and get her ready for school, so I got up with Chris. She rose early to exercise, and then took a shower, blew dry her hair, and made her breakfast, which she often did wearing only her underwear. "Aren't you cold?" I asked her one morning.

"Not really. I don't want to get food on my work clothes."

"How about a bathrobe?"

"Is there a problem?"

"No," I said. "Not really."

But there was a problem, although it was too hard to explain, even to myself. I didn't want to see so much of Chris's body. When she walked into the bedroom naked after her shower, I turned away. When she left the house for work, her shirt still unbuttoned enough to show her freckled chest, the edge of her bra, I tried not to see either. I told myself it was because there wasn't time, we were too busy, we were too tired. But this wasn't the truth. I didn't turn toward the body that used to stop me in my tracks because I didn't want to be stopped anymore.

I had been pregnant twice now; twice I had given birth, and now I was nursing again. And Chris's body had become a sort of fun-house mirror. These are your small hips, it seemed to say to me, your narrow ribcage, your firm belly. This is you and not you. This is your lover, who remains unchanged as you expand and contract, leak and bleed and ache. It was the wrong way to see Chris, and it kept me from her, kept me from receiving her desire, which I knew to be genuine, and yet I could not help myself. I thought often of men then, of crawling into bed with a person to whom I bore no resemblance so that I could lose, if only for a little while, the confusing burden of my body.

I complained to Kelly about what Chris wasn't doing, or what she was doing that I wish she weren't. I told her more than I had in the past, certainly more than I did when Grace was younger and Kelly was so vocal in her criticism of Chris's involvement. But I was no longer as interested in protecting Chris. So I complained and Kelly rolled her eyes; she laughed and commiserated. Which always—always—left me feeling worse. But I kept doing it. I can see now that the mistake I made was in thinking that the things Kelly could see were the things that mattered most.

"Do you ever think about having an affair?" Chris asked me one night when Kelly was sleeping over. I had come to bed late, thinking she was already asleep, and was startled by her question. It was a different question than she used to ask me, all those years ago when we first got together and she was worried that I was too inexperienced. "Do you want to date other women?" she would ask. "It's really fine with me." I would always say no. "You're asking because *you* want to," I would say. But this time I didn't think she was asking for permission.

"I think about having an affair with you," I said.

Chris kissed me then, and in a few minutes she was asleep. But I was awake, thinking about her question. Earlier that evening, when Kelly and I were talking about her trip to New York, she told me she had started leaving clothes in her girlfriend's apartment. "Just a few dresses and sweaters, you know. And I brought down some cookbooks, and some good sheets. I didn't like her sheets."

And it was those details, those benign domestic details, that made me want what Kelly had. I wanted a weekend in the apartment of someone who loved me and wanted my company and did not expect me to do things for her. I wanted to hang a few of my dresses in her closet, dresses that she would notice and like seeing me in, dresses that were not in a pile on the closet floor because who needs dresses when you are nursing a baby? I would have liked to bring my Julia Child so that we could make beef bourguignon on a long Sunday afternoon, an afternoon that was long because we had no obligations, not long because bedtime was still six hours away.

Remodel or Divorce

Lying in the dark next to Chris, listening to her sleep, I understood that it would be impossible to have an affair with her. Even if we could wrestle ourselves free of the girls, check in to a hotel and pull the shades, even then we would still be ourselves. The story of the girls and the work of them and our guilt, worry, and anger would still be written all over our bodies, still be heard under all our whispers, however desirous, however urgent. Chris could not ease my preoccupation, and she certainly could not ease my rage. No, an affair could only be with a body on which a new story could be told and a familiar one forgotten, if only for a little while.

The great thing about your life," a friend told me when I was pregnant with Grace, "is that you'll always be doing something radical. Even if you have a baby and stay home, you'll be doing it with a woman. You'll never feel mainstream."

My friend was wrong. I did feel mainstream—I was mainstream. But the difference was I was less inclined to do something about it—and more tolerant of my situation—because Chris and I were both women. I had bought into my friend's mythology; I had stayed quiet when straight friends had said that surely the domestic lives of same-sex couples were more equitable than their own. I had set myself apart, for no reason other than my lesbian marriage. But the truth was that having a wife didn't preclude me from being one.

Today I Saw God in the Face of a Kitten

W hy don't you go to church?" Chris suggested one Sunday morning when June was a few months old and I was in a bad mood. Every weekend during June's early babyhood Chris suggested I get out and do something. Why don't you take a walk?" she would say. "Why don't you get some coffee and read the paper?" She was really saying please take a break so you'll stop being mad at me.

I didn't want to stop being mad. I knew all about three deep breaths, about leaving the room or walking around the block, but I didn't want to do any of those things. My anger, when it really got going, was enlivening. It was almost sexual in its power, in its license. When I got angry enough I would allow myself to say terrible things that I didn't mean, but that were extraordinarily satisfying to say. I was reminded of something the Catholic writer Melissa Nussbaum once wrote about her young son when she told him that Jesus tells us not to hit people. "Jesus didn't like to hit," the little boy said. "But I do."

I also didn't want to take a break because I didn't want Chris to think she was settling the score. I felt profoundly owed a debt of hours that Chris could never pay back, and I didn't want her to think that by taking June for the afternoon or putting her down for a nap we would be even. It didn't occur to me that "getting even" was not what Chris had in mind at all.

"Hey hon," Chris said one Sunday morning when I had snapped at Grace for not putting away her shoes. "Would you please go to church?"

"You know West Cummington really isn't enough for me," I said, annoyed.

"It's better than nothing," she said.

"I'm not sure it is."

But I went. I went to West Cummington most every Sunday morning when June was a baby, because by Sunday morning even I had to admit that I really, really wanted to get out of the house, and I didn't so much care where I went. We had been members of West Cummington for as many years as we had lived in the hill-towns, and I knew that any sense of home I had was in large part because of the people I knew and loved at church. We were not typical hilltowners: we didn't raise animals or tap our maple trees or pickle anything. I didn't plan on homeschooling and I didn't knit. But at West Cummington those things didn't matter. We all drove the same rutted roads to that church on the hill; the same snow and mud covered the boots of everyone who pulled open the tall wooden door to the sanctuary on Sunday mornings.

June was usually sleepy when the service started at nine thirty, so I stood in the back of the sanctuary during announcements and the call to worship, shushing her, two-stepping her to sleep in the sling. If she didn't settle quickly, I slipped out the back door and walked along the ledge to the road until she settled, not worrying that she wouldn't. I could manage her in a way I hadn't been able to manage Grace; I could manage June alone in a way I could not yet manage both of them together. Motherhood expanded me the first time and again the second, so that when I was alone with June I felt a near-thrilling excess of competence.

Church was a welcome escape in those early months with June, a place to hear a sermon and sing shape-note hymns, to see people I loved. A place where June's slurpy nursing and my yoga pants were welcome. I didn't ask much more of those Sunday mornings. During moments of silence or prayers for the people, I didn't work to quiet my mind; I didn't talk to God. I kissed the top of June's warm head, I paged through the hymnal. I looked out the window at the greening hillside, the apple trees, the narrow road.

June was baptized in early summer, when she was three months old. A congregant who was pregnant with her own second child sang "Down by the River to Pray" and Steve doused June's head with creek water, as he had doused Grace's nearly four years before. He read from *To Kill a Mockingbird* because June's middle name was Harper, and he preached to everyone about the burdens and glories of parenthood. During the baptism he asked, "By what name will this child be known?" and Grace, who was in my arms, said, "Junebug." I thanked God for the glories of two daughters, of sisters. I did not think of Father Dowling.

St. Rumi's was Chris's nickname for West Cummington, and it was an apt one. West Cummington was ecumenical to its core; Steve sought and plumbed connections between texts, across continents, languages, and centuries. And he did it with an integrity that I could see even when it annoyed me, even when I hungered for him to simply talk about Jesus. On the seemingly rare occasions when he did, just the word coming out of his mouth stirred me— stirred in me, and I would startle, I would shift my attention from the window, from June's body. Jesus. I would feel alive and alone, in the best possible way. I would be reminded that I was a believer, although more than even that I would be reminded that I was seen, and I was loved.

There was something else that stirred me during those mornings in church, something that turned my attention away from the view, and from June. After the sermon and the offering Steve led the congregation in prayer, which was a solemn few moments of petition when people were invited to say aloud the names of people who were "sick, suffering, or numb, in body, mind, or spirit." Some weeks only a few people whispered a name or two, other weeks the litany was long. I knew many of the people whose names were called out, although I often did not know of their troubles. Every week I whispered Chris's name. Not because she was sick, suffering, or numb, but because when I thought of God's attention, of God's loving hand, I thought of Chris. I think now what I was saying when I whispered her name was, please turn me toward her, because I can't seem to turn toward her myself.

All summer, June and I spent Sunday mornings at West Cummington. Sometimes I stood in the back with another mother, her baby also in a sling. We shared a hymnal and whispered through the service like schoolgirls, but by Labor Day, June could no longer fall asleep in my arms at church. She needed a nap in her crib, and when she woke she needed to make noise and eat mashed avocados. So I started leaving her at home with Chris and Grace and going to church by myself. It should have been a luxury to go without June, and sometimes it was. But going without her meant that she and her sister were mine for the rest of the day. And even harder than cashing in all my child-free time was sitting alone in the pew without a head to kiss, a tiny slinged backside to pat. When I was there with June I was worshipping her—her tiny, quiet body, her full lips pressed against my chest.

But when I wasn't in church with June I wanted church to be more, to do more. I wanted the Eucharist and I wanted Jesus, every single week. I wanted to emerge from church feeling well traveled, rinsed clean. But West Cummington could only be what it had always been: a modest country church filled with my neighbors. "Today I saw God in the face of a kitten," a woman with a brusque voice and a gray ponytail announced on one of the first Sundays Chris and I went to West Cummington together. We laughed for years about that line, and while no one ever said anything quite so absurd again, church was still filled with the news and noise of our small town, and there was no pageantry there. Nor was there meant to be: the point of that Sunday morning gathering was not to exalt but rather to pause and take notice of gratitude and grief, or of the complicated ordinary that sleeps between. And I could do that when there was a baby in my arms, but I couldn't do it without her. So sometime during the winter before June turned one I stopped going to church. An old longing began to bloom again, a longing that at the time I might have said was a longing for God. But I believe now that it was really more than that. It was grief for someone I did not, and would not now become.

A few weeks after June's first birthday, we left her with a babysitter and drove to Worcester for Chris's niece's first communion. The church was familiar to me now: after Chris's grandparents' funerals all those years ago we had returned together several times. First for her niece's baptism, a quiet service for which the family stood gathered around the baptismal font, all of us trying not to laugh as the baby blew spit bubbles down her white gown while the priest asked her godparents to guide her in her renunciation of Satan. And we had also come for our nephew's first communion. I spent most of the service at the preschool playground with a wily, eighteen-month-old Grace. I brought her into the sanctuary's entryway during the communion rites so I could watch, but I became distracted by an antichoice poster that hung on the wall near the door. "Stop the killing of innocent babies," it said. I took a marker out of Grace's bag of toys and added "IN IRAQ!!!" in large block letters.

As we were leaving, I showed Chris. "I did that," I whispered, pointing to the poster. "Nice," she whispered back. I felt a surge of connection to her then, which pleased me, because otherwise we were at odds in church, over the Church, although we never spoke of it. See, I was saying to her then, I agree with you. Mostly.

At our niece's first communion, the sanctuary was packed with families, squirming babies in tights with bows taped to their heads, fathers with video cameras. Grace couldn't believe the girls' dresses, their veils. "Why does it look like they're getting married?" she asked.

"Bride of Christ," Chris whispered, rolling her eyes. I gave her a look.

"They're just really dressed up," I said. "It's a very special occasion. You don't have to wear a veil."

"I did," Chris said. Grace and I both ignored her.

"Do I get to wear one to Steve's church?"

"I don't think so," I said. "We don't really do first communion. You can take communion whenever you want."

West Cummington was the only church Grace had known, and she was accustomed to Steve, in his Carhartts and sandals and, on special occasions, linen sports coat. She was accustomed to white walls and two candles and a vase of flowers from someone's garden, and she certainly had never seen Jesus hanging on the cross, although she didn't mention him, and I didn't point him out.

I liked being back in that church, although I hardly felt like I *was* in church. The service was busy and distracting, lots of chatting between pews, leaning up or back to talk with a cousin or old friend in a loud whisper, which I—now a beloved member of the family—thoroughly enjoyed. But it didn't leave much time to think about where I was, how I felt being in a Catholic church after all this time. And then it was time for communion, and I didn't know what to do. I hesitated, and when it came time for the people in our pew to join the line, I sat back, gave them space to pass by me.

Today I Saw God in the Face of a Kitten   147

Later Grace asked me why I didn't go up for communion. "Mati told me she wouldn't go, but you would. But then you didn't."

"Oh," I said, trying not to sound as surprised, as flustered as I was. "Not this time." It was a dismissive answer, but what else could I say? Chris had told Grace I would receive communion? Had I known that, had I known her expectation, her allowance for me, I would have gone up. But why did I need her permission? Why was it for her to decide if my involvement in the Church—however occasional, however peripheral—was acceptable, was not a threat to our marriage? Over the past several years I had packed away most of the relics of my Catholicism. I kept my grandmother's rosary beads, but I let Grace wear them with her dress-up clothes. I read Andre Dubus and Flannery O'Connor, but not Thomas Merton. I had devised a sort of calculus whereby I allowed just enough Catholicism into my consciousness to keep me from acknowledging how much of it I had lost.

A few days after the service in Worcester, we were at the kitchen counter, reading the paper. Chris was reading aloud to me about something the Church had done or said. I don't remember what it was, perhaps a statement against gay marriage or a condemnation of a secretly ordained female priest. Or maybe it was something less serious, like a pair of four-hundred-dollar Prada shoes owned by the pope. (Chris was constantly reporting to me on the antics of the pope. I couldn't seem to make her understand that he meant nothing to me.)

"I'm sorry," she said—although we both knew that she was not—"but I can't understand how anyone could be a part of club based on bigotry and exclusion. How could anyone belong to a church that says her life is a sin?"

I knew Chris well enough to know that this was not so much an invitation to conversation as it was an inquisition. Did I feel this way? Was I going to join her in full renunciation of the Church? Would I, once and for all, wash my hands of these men and their bigotry, their cowardice?

Instead I asked her a question. "Does it ever make you sad," I asked, "that you gave it up?" And before she could answer, I asked what was, for me, the real question. "Do you ever miss it?"

"No," she said. "I don't miss anything about it."

And then I knew that when we had these conversations we were not talking about the same thing, we were not talking about the same thing at all.

But this was what I did not yet understand: if we weren't talking about belief, if we weren't talking about God, it wasn't because of Chris. It was because of me. She would have talked about belief with me, if I had the courage to talk about it. But I didn't even have the vocabulary. Not anymore. I wanted to fault her for her focus on the Church's exclusionary policies, but in truth we were both reacting to them. She was fighting, and I was giving up. It was easier for me to miss God and the Church than it was to think that I—like all gay people—had been hurt by a straight person who saw my desires as incompatible with a faithful life. And because I couldn't acknowledge that prejudice I couldn't move past it, or perhaps I should say I couldn't move back from it, back to the months of early belief and the happiness it brought me. It was easier for me to live without God than it was to admit my gayness, my otherness, and the way it had ushered me out of the world of ease and privilege I had been born into. We talked about the Church because I couldn't talk about God; we talked about the pope because I couldn't talk about Hector. We talked about four-hundred-dollar shoes because I could not say to Chris, "Look: I loved that crazy Church, I loved those wild ideas about God, and I gave them up because I also wanted you."

The Memory ┃ 18
of Hunger

On a Saturday afternoon in winter, when the sun was not shining and hadn't shone in weeks, we got a babysitter for the girls—now five and nearly two years old—and drove to the new tapas bar in town. We thought tapas might warm us up, but the restaurant, with its black-lacquer tables and bright murals of tropical flowers and fish, felt cold. After we sat down, the waitress brought us sangria and a plate of dates wrapped in bacon. While we looked at the menus, Chris asked, laughing, "Remember how hungry you were in Spain?"

I remembered. The summer before we were married we went to San Sebastián on the northern coast of Spain, and during the week we spent there I invariably became hungry at the precise times of day when there was no food to be found. So I ate bags of cherries on the beach while the shop owners napped the afternoon away; in early evening I ate toasted bread slathered with mayonnaise and anchovies at cheap tapas bars while some of Europe's finest restaurant kitchens were still hours from opening for dinner.

But my hunger was not what I thought of when I remembered San Sebastián. Sitting across from Chris now, drinking sangria even though it was much too cold outside for sangria, I was remembering the towering statue of Jesus that stood atop Monte Urgull, one of the two small mountains that formed San Sebastián's crescent-shaped harbor. I could see the statue everywhere I went in San Sebastián, from the beach where we swam without bathing suit tops, from our hotel room, from the streets I walked in search of a café that would serve lunch at two o'clock. I loved the statue more than I could say, and all week I thought: if only I lived here! If only I could look up, at any moment of the day, and see him, robed arms extended, in any light and any season, against clouds or brilliant coastal sun, through rain, through mist, through wet flakes of snow. Then it would be impossible for days—for weeks—to go by in the way they did now, without a single thought of him.

How could we remember such different things? I asked myself, suddenly angry. The real question—the question I didn't yet know to ask myself—was how could she remember what I had never told her?

I looked at Chris and didn't know her. She was the far coast, rising to a different dawn, to a view I did not know and had long ago stopped trying to imagine. I want you closer! I wanted to say, but couldn't. I opened my mouth to speak and faltered. She looked at me expectantly. "What is it?" she asked.

"You don't do enough," I blurted out. "I need more help. With the kids, with the house, with everything. You don't do enough, and it's making me miserable."

Chris's face hardened. "So am I," she said. "When we get home, I think you should start looking for a job. Get out of the house. That way I could finally work less."

I was stunned. I hadn't meant to get us here—oh, how I hadn't meant to get us here, here to this place where I always got us! But I wasn't going to back down.

"Good idea," I said. "Good idea."

"You know," she said with a harsh smile, "our life is like that Ethan Hawke line in *Before Sunset*, 'We used to be married and now we're two people who run a childcare center together.'"

I took a long drink, emptying my sangria glass. I hated few things as much as I hated her quoting that line, which she did with infuriating regularity. I hated the line because Ethan Hawke says it to a woman who is not his wife (and with whom he is about to have sex); I hated it because I was the one running the damn childcare, not Chris.

But this time I was so angry I decided to agree with her. "Exactly," I said. "That's exactly who we are." And then I began to cry so hard that it became clear we couldn't stay in the restaurant. And even if I could have stopped, there was no point in staying—the date was ruined. Chris told me to go wait outside while she paid the check. I bumped the edge of the table as I got up; my drink spilled, my napkin fell to the floor, but I kept walking.

I pushed open the door and pulled on my coat. I had been sweating in the restaurant and now I was freezing and shivery and still crying. I walked across the street to our car and saw that our parking meter had expired. I didn't know if I should put more money in it—I had no idea where we were going now, or what we were going to do. I started to open my purse, to rummage its depths for quarters. And then suddenly, in one instant, I understood the strangest thing, and I understood it completely: the way to Chris was not toward Chris. It was toward everything I turned away from so that I could love her. And for a moment, a moment that I can only know as grace, this fact didn't frighten me. And by the time it did, I understood it clearly enough to know that, frightening or not, it had become an entirely inevitable truth.

And then Chris was next to me. "Let's drive somewhere," I said, and without waiting for her I got into the driver's seat and turned on the car. She got in, and I turned up the heat and drove us slowly, on ice-rutted roads, to a neighborhood near the restaurant. We got out of the car and when we were both on the sidewalk I looked at Chris. "I like my life," I said. "I do. But it's not enough."

Chris nodded. She didn't ask me to explain and I didn't try to.

"Let's walk," I said. And then I bent my head, because I was crying and couldn't stop and didn't want to explain why.

She held out her hand for me, and I took it. The sidewalks were snow-packed and icy, and I leaned into her with each step, and for the first time in a long while I relaxed against her solid and unyielding body.

I had been jealous of Chris, jealous, I told myself, of her career, her confidence, her closet full of suits and her good haircut. But what I really wanted was Chris's wholeness, the way that everything that mattered to her made it into her life and her days. Even the things she longed for but couldn't have were always in her mind and our conversations; they were in the books on her bedside table and the movies she watched late at night. She was not afraid of what she wanted, even those things she could not have because she had a wife and children now.

It was true that I wanted the things we fought over. I wanted her to take the kids more, and to appreciate all the housework I did, in the same way she wanted me to offer some thanks that she went to work every day. Our arrangement was a risky one, with many faults. But we could weather that. What we could no longer weather was my secret longing, my aging grief over the God I had given up for Chris. We could no longer weather my tired and childish longing for a towering statue to remind me of what I believed. The remembering was up to me.

Easter | 19

A month later, in the coldest hours of a January night, the West Cummington Church burned to the ground. A fire started in the furnace and set the nearly two-hundred-year-old wooden church ablaze. The fire department contained the fire but the building was destroyed. The water from the fire hoses ran down the road like a river and froze.

The work parties began in the spring and volunteers spent long afternoons pulling every last nail from the few timbers that remained so that they could be planed and used in the new church that would be built right on those ruins. I didn't go to the work parties. Every time I drove on the road below Church Hill I looked up and saw that there was nothing there, nothing where there was once the most eternal, most seemingly permanent something. The absence of the church was like an optical illusion. It was like magic. It was like death.

All spring when I would run into people I hadn't seen in a long time they would offer condolences about the church. I heard about your church, they would say, how terrible, how sad. Yes, I would say, it is, it was. I felt guilty when I thanked people for their sympathies. Aside from Christmas Eve, I had not been in the West Cummington Church for nearly a year before it burned. I was as far away from it as I had ever been.

The Easter after the fire, I didn't go to church, even though services were still being held, at the Parish House down the hill from the site of the old church. Instead we lingered through the morning's egg hunt, and in the late afternoon we went to the house of our friends Cyndy and Hanno for dinner.

I was standing at the kitchen sink when their five-year-old daughter, Greta, walked into the room and asked, "Is anyone here a Christian?" The kitchen was filled with girls and their mothers. Some of the girls were wearing eyeliner for the first time; one of them—June—was just a toddler. The girls were sitting at the counter eating shrimp dumplings and drinking passion-fruit juice while we—their mothers—cooked and drank gin and snuck chocolate eggs from their Easter baskets. From the window over the sink I could see their fathers—and Chris—building a fire to roast lamb and hot dogs and, when the flames were low enough, marshmallow peeps.

"I am not," said Michele, the mother of an eye-lined girl. "I am an agnostic."

I turned from the sink to look at Greta. "Do you know what agnostic means?" I asked her. She shook her head. Michele started to explain but Greta slid from her bar stool before Michele could finish. Greta grabbed Grace's arm and a moment later I saw both of them run across the grass toward the fire.

"Our Seder was last night," Cyndy explained, "and it's a lot, you know? Greta wants to know: Am I a Jew or am I a Christian? She gets Passover, but what does she really know about Easter? I want to give it to her right; I want to tell her about the resurrection and the ascension; I want to show her the paintings. I want her to have the big Catholic myth."

I smiled at Cyndy, but I didn't say anything. June, no longer content to sit on a big girl's lap, was crying for me. I wiped my hands on my skirt and reached for her. She was tired and her face was sticky from chocolate and dumplings. I sat her on the counter next to the sink, put a stockpot under the tap, and let it fill with cold water. I turned and held up my glass when Cyndy walked past me with the cocktail shaker; I took a bite of a dumpling and offered the rest to June, who ate it from my fingers.

Greta came back inside, breathless from her sprint across the lawn. She smelled like fire and melting snow. I wanted to tell her I was a Christian. I'm a Christian, I wanted to say, and do you know what that means? It means that I believe Jesus is the child of God, and that he loves justice and he loves us, and he wants us to see God in each other.

But I didn't tell Greta anything. I was in my own promised land, right there in that kitchen filled with dear and kindred friends, friends who had not been easy to find. How could I say such an unexpected thing to these women with whom I shared my life now, this life of bodies and logistics and day following day following day? They knew what I thought about night nursing and homeschooling and the last season of *Friday Night Lights*, but they didn't know anything about what I believed, or what I called myself. How strange, I thought, that what I believe suddenly seems, as it did all those years ago in Philadelphia, like the only thing that really matters at all.

There was no church on the hill anymore, but there was still Steve, and so a few days after Easter I paid him a visit. The windows in his office were open to the sounds of birdcall and the river, and the two-lane highway beyond. The office was small: there was room for a desk, a few chairs, and an OED, open on a stand. We talked about small things, about the girls and about the goings-on in the town around us. We talked—as we were all beginning to talk then—about the new fame of our neighbor Rachel Maddow.

After a few minutes I began to explain to Steve why I had called him the day before and asked for a meeting. And when I did, I began to cry. Through my tears I told Steve how much I loved the West Cummington Church, but that I was afraid it was not quite right for me, that I needed something else, that I needed the Catholic Church, which I loved once and might still love, but was a million miles from me now. I told him how impossible it was to be married to a woman, to have two children with her, and to still find a home in the Catholic Church. This might have sounded like the excuse I offered to him all those years ago when I was pregnant with Grace, but in reality it was the opposite, perhaps because now I believed it to be true.

"I could go," I said, wiping my teary cheeks with the back of my hand, "if we had some sort of different life, you know, if we lived in a city"—and here, even in the moment, I knew that I was entering into some world of childish and magical thinking—"if I could walk out of our house on a Sunday morning and down the block to the Catholic Church." I was articulating, consciously or not, the fantasy of returning to my basement chapel, to the easy closeness of it, the familiarity of its stone steps, its dark pews and chipping statues. The fantasy of a free and faithful young self.

"If I could be part of it again," I continued, "even in the smallest way, so that I could see if it was where I really belonged."

"You don't need a different life," Steve said, kindly calling my bullshit. "Turn right at the bottom of the hill some Sunday morning and drive yourself to the Catholic Church."

"And what will I tell Chris?" I asked him, immediately wishing I hadn't.

"That this is who you are and what you need," he said. "Or, you will tell her nothing."

Steve didn't ask why I didn't want to tell Chris. Even if he had, I wouldn't have known what to say. Not yet, at least. I had not, until this moment, allowed myself to acknowledge that Hector was not the only person who believed my love for Chris and my love for Catholicism were incompatible. Chris believed it too.

Easter　　　157

We talked for a few more minutes, and then Steve walked me to my car. "I read something about Mary Oliver once," he said, "something about her showing up late for dinner at a friend's house—really late—and when she finally arrived, she told them that a poem had caught her, and she had to sit down at her desk and write. She told them not to worry about her if she were late again, or even if she failed to show up completely. She would be fine; she would be doing something essential. When I read that, I thought, well that's pretty self-involved of her." Steve laughed, rolling his eyes. "But as I thought about it more I came to genuinely admire her devotion." He looked at me, so kindly. "I'm glad you came today," he said, "so that when I don't see you here, I will know why, and I won't worry."

On Sunday morning I turned right at the bottom of the hill. I drove to St. Elizabeth's in Northampton, where I entered though the side door and found a seat near the back. I kicked down the kneeler and went gently onto my knees.

During the service I watched a woman in the pew in front of mine, a pretty woman dressed in khaki shorts, a thin, white sweater over her shoulders. She didn't sing (no one sang, really, although I did, loudly); she didn't respond to the responsorial Psalms. She rose and knelt at the appropriate times; she gently embraced her husband during the passing of the peace. I stood behind her in the communion line and as she approached the priest she took a small gold box from her pocket, opened the latch, and held it in her hands. The priest put one host in her box and one in her open palm. She ate the host from her hand and then closed her box, put it back in her pocket. Who would she deliver it to, I wondered? Who was too sick, too fragile to come here and receive for herself? I thought of Nana on her sunporch, and the woman who brought the Eucharist to her that Easter morning. And then it was my turn to hold out my hand. I wished I also had a box. It was enviable, this chance to lock the host away. To save it. But I only had my hand, and for a moment I thought of keeping the host until I got back to my pew, then slipping it carefully into my bag. But I didn't. With my tongue I pushed it against the roof of my mouth, where it began to dissolve, and then was gone.

Sisters of Wisdom   20

As a child I had one Catholic friend. Her name was Denise. In second grade Denise bragged about her first communion dress, which I coveted. (Decades later the Catholic girls in my own daughters' second-grade classes would brag about *their* first communion dresses, which my daughters would also covet.) Denise had something else I adored: a stack of cards on her dining room table printed with red roses and the words "All Life Is Precious," in curling cursive script. "You can have one," Denise said, holding up her finger in case I didn't understand what the word "one" meant. How I loved that card. I knew it was somehow connected to the "Abortion Stops a Beating Heart" bumper sticker on Denise's wood-paneled station wagon, but I wasn't entirely sure how. I also loved Denise's mother, who had short, graying hair and thick black glasses. She was from "back east" and talked much more loudly than other girls' moms. She insisted Denise go to CCD and later that she become an altar girl, obligations Denise found taxing but I thought seemed rather exciting.

Twice a year Denise's mother went on retreat to a monastery in the mountains. When I asked Denise what her mother did on retreat, she said, "Oh, she talks to God. And priests." Once I happened to be at Denise's house when her mother returned from her two days in the mountains with God and priests. Her face was terribly sunburned. "I fell asleep!" she said, her hands to her cheeks. "In the sun, on a stone bench. I was praying and then I was asleep. I slept for four hours! I was in heaven."

I thought of Denise's mother when I checked in for a three-day retreat at Wisdom House, an interfaith retreat center in the Berkshires. I wasn't there to talk to priests, and maybe not even to talk to God. But I did want to fall asleep on a stone bench in the sun, depite the fact that it was only May in chilly New England. I wanted that heaven.

"May I sit here?" I asked a table of gray-haired nuns at my first dinner. I was uncertain of the protocol, the seating arrangements. It had been a long time since my own dining hall years. In those days it was three glasses of water, cottage cheese on my salad. Now it was quinoa-stuffed peppers and baked cod.

"Please, please," the women said in unison. I knew these women were nuns because the nun who showed me to my room told me as much, and I also knew because, quite honestly, they looked like nuns. No habits, but gray hair dominated, as did sensible shoes and simple cross pendants hanging low over cardigans and collared sweatshirts.

"Are you here for the workshop?" the woman sitting next to me asked.

"Oh, no," I said. "I'm here on my own."

Someone asked about my family, and I told them I had two young daughters. "Where are they this weekend?" one asked.

"At home," I said.

"Weekend with Dad," one of them said with a smile.

"Actually with Mom," I said. "I'm married to a woman." I didn't always correct people's mistaken assumptions about my sexual orientation. But there were two circumstances in which I always did: when I was with the girls, and when I wanted the person who made the assumption to know exactly who I was.

If my correction was troubling to any of these women they did not let on.

Before that first dinner was over it was clear to me that these were not ordinary women. One was a sculptor and accomplished fiddle player; one a high school theater teacher; and another had returned, that afternoon, from a year's mission in the Northwest Territories. She told us that the previous morning at dawn someone came bearing a caribou to the rectory she shared with a Jesuit priest, and they butchered the animal together on the long kitchen table. "My mission up there was being," she said. "I was there to live, to witness, and today, back here," she said with a sad smile, "I am a bit adrift. What will I be called to do? Something wonderful, certainly, but right now I have no idea what that is."

The nuns spent that first dinner catching up. Those who didn't live together knew each other from other retreats, other projects. Who signed the protest letter, one wanted to know, about the Vatican investigation of American nuns? All of them. One asked when another friend would arrive. "Oh, I didn't know she was coming!" the woman next to me said. "I haven't seen her since last summer when she made us all jump off that dock."

After our meals together, the nuns went to their workshops and I went back to my little room and wrote. I also read, and did a little yoga, and lay on the small bed listening to the rain. I had no specific goal for the retreat; I only wanted to step outside my life for a little while, to make a space. A clearing. Those three days were the longest time I had ever spent away from June, who was now two years old. I hardly ever went away without the girls. When Grace was nearly two, I spent twenty-four hours alone in a hotel, where I read magazines in the bath, brought a novel to dinner, and awoke at four in the morning with a terrible pain in my breasts. Who knew a twenty-month-old could still commission so much breast milk? A few months later I left a fully weaned Grace and flew to Washington, DC, for the weekend. When my friend picked me up at the airport she told me that she wanted to have a baby someday just so she could leave her for the weekend and look as happy as I did. Chris had been leaving the girls since they were infants, and not only for work. Only I traveled alone with the girls; often I took them away for a week or longer, leaving Chris at home by herself, at home to enjoy the peace of a childless house where she could sleep as late as she pleased on Sunday morning and spend the afternoon on the couch with a book. "You never take them away," I would say to her when I returned from these trips, suitcases full of dirty laundry, exhausted from the strain of entertaining two children on a plane. "I never get to be alone in the house."

I was caught up in a great reckoning then, trying to even a scale that was never going to strike middle. Middle was simply not where our marriage was going to rest. I was beginning, in that time when I went to Wisdom House, to understand that seeking the elusive middle was my own folly. My contentment lay in seeking something else.

But what I first learned at Wisdom House was that I was tired. I lay down to read and woke hours later, the book open across my chest. I sat down to write and fought to stay awake, although I didn't fight too hard. Instead I went outside, tried to rouse myself with long walks in the woods and along country roads lined with well-kept houses and stone walls far sturdier than the nearly ancient and crumbling ones that wound through our woods. When I came in from walking I wandered around Wisdom House, read the posters that lined the walls about the lives of nuns: nuns in El Salvador, nuns among migrant workers, nuns who wrote poems, taught in jails, held vigils at nuclear reactors and in old-growth forests. I spent many hours in the library and also the bookstore, sitting on the floor with a pile of books next to me. The books brought a familiar feeling back to me, that intoxicating possibility of salvation through words. But I couldn't concentrate long enough to read more than a chapter or two of any of them. I was always wanting to get back to the dining hall, back to the nuns.

In the dining hall I often found myself sitting next to the sculptor from the Bronx, whose name was Peggy. She always asked me how the writing was going, asked how my girls were doing without me. "Fine, fine," I said. I didn't want to talk about either. I wanted to listen. And I also wanted to project myself into a make-believe future when these women were my friends, when I would travel to New York to see them, to see their work and their schools, to show them my daughters. To tell them my story and listen to them tell me how to be a different kind of Catholic in the world. This is it, I thought, more than once. This is what I have been waiting for.

At lunch on Sunday I exchanged email addresses with Peggy. We hugged good-bye, and I went upstairs to pack my things. It was a bright and warming day—the rain had finally stopped—and I was not ready to go home. I drove the few miles from Wisdom House to the Lourdes of Litchfield Grotto. The benches around the grotto were filled with people wearing sunglasses and comfortable shoes. Some had cameras around their necks. I didn't linger. Instead I followed a wooden arrow pointing to the Stations of the Cross.

Years ago Chris and I stopped in the town of San Luis in southern Colorado because I wanted to see its famous Stations of the Cross. The high desert sun heated the trail's pebbly switchbacks and so we barely paused when we reached each small iron station. In milder weather I could have lingered at each one; they were beautiful in their dark and metallic harshness. At the top of the mountain there was a small shrine, a sun-faded statue of Mary surrounded by small, turquoise-colored stones. Some of the stones had spilled over onto the path and I picked one up and slipped it into the pocket of my cutoff shorts. Chris started walking down ahead of me. I didn't want to go. There was a feeling that I did not want to end, and it was not a comfortable feeling, necessarily. It was a sense of approach, of proximity to something that I needed and wanted, something that wanted me.

My visit to Lourdes of Litchfield was not so complicated. The statues were towering and theatrical and a little too realistically rendered. But they were also beautiful, as was the jewel-green hillside that surrounded them. At the last station a couple and their young daughter were planting pansies at the disciples' feet. When I circled back to the grotto I felt no need to stay. I had seen enough, and I knew it. I happily attributed this peaceful certainty to my weekend at Wisdom House, to the possibility I felt when I sat with Peggy and all the others.

The next week I sent Peggy an email. I told her all the things I didn't tell her when we were there together: that I was once a practicing Catholic but had not been since I was married, that I now belonged to a small Congregational church but was not sure it was quite right for me. That I missed the Church. What I didn't tell her was that I wanted her in my life. I wanted her to be my nun. Peggy wrote back the next morning, and when I opened the email I was immediately disappointed. It was too short. Three lines, to be exact. Those three lines, before I even read them, told me that Peggy and I were not going to be friends, that she was not going to invite me to her house in the Bronx to drink tea with her and her fellow nuns around their wooden kitchen table. Those three lines told me that Peggy was not going to be my nun.

Dear Erin, she wrote, *I know a priest in Boston you might want to talk to. Your church sounds like a good one. I'll keep you in my prayers.*

Between God and Me   21
There Is No Me

I'm going to Boston next week," I said to Chris on a June night a few weeks after I had returned home from Wisdom House. Both girls were in bed, and I had just received an email from Peggy's priest, whose name was Ron Ingalls. I had written to him first, to ask for a visit. He had written right back. "Of course," he said. "How about next week?"

"What for?" Chris asked.

"I'm going to see a priest."

Chris looked surprised. "Really?"

I tried to seem casual, like it was no big deal. "He's a friend of one of the nuns I met at that residency. He sounds kind of amazing," I said. "He does same-sex weddings, and heads this really liberal congregation. And he's married."

"Then how is he a priest?" Chris asked.

"Well, officially he left the Church," I explained, "but he's still a Catholic priest."

"How is that possible?"

I was getting exasperated. "Because he was ordained, and he believes in the sacraments, and he wants to serve believing people, I guess."

Chris looked confused. "I guess I don't see how that would work," she said.

"It's not really the point," I said. "The point is, I'm going to see a priest next week."

"Because?"

"Because of Hector," I said without thinking. I looked at Chris then, and I wondered if she even knew who I was talking about.

"Oh," she said. "Got it."

I began to say something else, to explain more of what I was doing, to qualify it, but I stopped. The way to Chris is not toward her. "I'll need to leave early," I said. "I'll need you to drop off the girls."

The next week I drove to Boston, to Ron's small house, where he kept an office. He opened the door and greeted me, smiling, his face thin and lively, his silver hair combed back from his face. "I'll warn you," he told me when we sat down, "I like to talk. Maybe you should tell me about yourself first."

But I didn't want to talk about myself, and so I asked him to start. He told me about his years in seminary and the years he spent in Baltimore as a young priest with a young congregation, and about the excitement he felt for the changes that Vatican II would bring, and the profound disappointment he felt when those changes did not come. He left the priesthood and married but continued to lead a small congregation of progressive Catholics and taught Latin and philosophy at a prestigious Boston high school.

There were some things Ron already knew about me, things that I had told him in an email a few weeks before our meeting. He knew that I was married to a woman and we had two children, and that a long time ago I was a practicing Catholic, sort of.

"So, then." I was having trouble deciding where to begin my story, how to present myself. Tell him what you were looking for, I told myself. What you are looking for now. I began to explain why I sought the Catholic Church, and after a moment I realized I didn't have much to say. The words coming out of my mouth seemed to belong to someone else, which is not to say that they were untrue, just unfamiliar. They sounded young and shallow, like one first gulp of air after another that can't seem to settle into the sustaining evenness of breath. Ron looked at me kindly; when I paused he didn't speak.

This is what I could not say, what I could not then put into words: I once loved—and will love for the entirety of my life—the Catholic imagination, which insists that the world is a mysterious and holy place, every corner, every instant ripe with the possibility of miracles. A crucifix hanging over an unmade bed, a kitchen windowsill lined with sun-faded Mass cards. Our Lady of the Angels, St. Mary's of the Snow. My young forehead tipped to receive holy water from my nana's fingertips. Blessings on the garden and the animals, the sleeping baby, the rising bread.

"Communion," I said finally, "is what I love."

Ron smiled. "It's ancient, isn't it? Our desire to share a meal. Every year we drive, we fly, we stop everything so that we can be together with the people we love around the Thanksgiving table. We want to gather, we want to share in the literal and symbolic feast."

I asked Ron about his congregation and he spoke about them, and about celebrating Mass, with enthusiasm. But he was also moving in new directions. He was clearly captivated by Eastern religions; he was interested in Buddhism and in meditation, in an examination of consciousness. "A friend of mine likes to say that between God and me there is no between," he said. "And for years I loved that. But now I like to say between God and me there is no me."

I decided to tell Ron about everything, and everyone, between God and me. I told him about St. Patrick's, and Father Dowling. I told him about Father Dowling's response to my nonconfession of having a girlfriend.

"Well, at least he wasn't hostile," Ron said. "I guess that's something." I could tell by his tone that he didn't actually think it was much of anything.

And I told him about Hector. Not the whole story, not exactly, but I told him about Hector's enthusiasm for my faith and his disapproval of my love affair, and the complications of both.

"You made the right decision," Ron said emphatically. "God is on the side of love." And then he added, "But you don't need me to tell you that."

"Actually," I said and then I stopped and for a moment neither one of us said anything. I smiled at Ron. "No," I said, "I don't."

It was so lovely to sit there with Ron in his office, an impressive poster of the Buddha on the wall above his head, a delicate statue of Mary on the table next to him. It was so lovely to hear a man talk about his enduring dedication to Catholicism and in the same breath his certainty that I was beloved. I had waited so long for this moment.

But then I looked at Ron, and perhaps it was the way his eyes were fixed on me, or the familiar distance between his chair and the couch where I sat, smoothing my skirt over my knees, but suddenly I knew that this was not something I could do again. I could not sit across from a gray-haired man and tell him my secrets because I wanted to know God. There couldn't be another Hector. Oh, but it's not the same! I told myself. Ron sees you—all of you—and believes in your goodness. You're not asking to be the exception. And I wasn't. But still, I had been here before. I had rested in the authority of others, and in their high regard for my intellect and faith, and in every meeting, every session, I had lost something. Or maybe it wasn't what I lost so much as what I absorbed: someone else's vision, someone else's articles of faith. Someone else's ideas about love. I would need to shed them now and begin to forge my own.

"I should go," I said, not wanting to leave but knowing I needed to. Knowing it was time. "I have a long drive, and I have to pick up my daughters." Ron walked me to the door, told me that he was here if I want to talk again, or we could email. Whatever I wanted. I thanked him, shook his hand, said good-bye.

I haven't seen Ron Ingalls since that day, although I think of him often. I think of him every time I say the words *be still and know that I am God*, and I say those words nearly every day. Ron is the person who told me that those words are the perfect meditation because each word, on its own, is a prayer. Because I am so often interrupted, so easily distracted, sometimes a word or two is all I can manage. But even a word changes things.

And I think of Ron when, every once in a while, I pick up a book by Richard Rohr. "Read him," Ron told me, "and you will be changed." I first opened one of Rohr's books on a quiet afternoon, stretched out on my bed while June lay next to me watching *Little Bear* on my laptop. *The story of our lives with God is a story of descent, not of ascent*, I read. I put down the book, closed my eyes. All right then, I thought. I'll descend, or at least I'll try. And I was not frightened, although I had been frightened for so many years. For so many years I had been certain that such a descent meant relinquishing the woman I loved, turning away from everything and everyone else I wanted. But I had been wrong. It was true that the Catholic Church could not be mine. I could not raise my children in it; I would not sit in the first pew and watch my daughters, their dresses as white as cake frosting, make their first communion. But this denial—real and painful as it was—did not mean I could not descend; it did not mean that if I wanted to move toward God I had to move alone. In the years since St. Patrick's I had made promises and forged bonds—forged bodies—from which I could never be fully separated. Before I knew Chris, before we had our children, the questions were: Who will come to me? Who will come and share this life? Those questions have been answered. And I could not, and would not, go anywhere without them.

After a few chapters I closed Rohr's book, rolled over on my side, and tried to smooth June's hair before she swatted away my hand, but, as always, she was too fast for me. I laughed and rolled over on my back with the closed book on my chest. I thought of

Ron's church in Wellesley, Peggy's house in the Bronx. Merton's Gethsemane. The basement chapel at St. Patrick's. All of them lovely, none of them meant for me.

This is what happens, still: I see a photograph in the newspaper of robed Christian Pilgrims in a Spanish cathedral or I find my rosary beads in a drawer when I am looking for a tape measure, and my heart beats faster. I can feel it. Still these things set me off. But now I know that all the beating of my heart means is that I need to stop for a moment and talk to God, to forget about the tape measure and the rosary beads, the pile of newspapers, and say something, anything. To close the distance. To remind myself that what I long for is something I can have.

For many, many years I kept that leather-bound book Hector gave me on my confirmation night. *The Imitation of Christ*. The book traveled with me to Colorado and back, from one apartment to the next, and then to Massachusetts, to the house where Chris and I were married in the living room, the house where I walked the halls in the night with a baby, twice over. It was an ordinary day when I finally let go of the book, an ordinary day when there was not enough room on the bookshelf and I cleared out what I didn't want: the airplane novels, the baby food cookbooks, the back issues of *Granta*. I tossed the book into the box with all the others, and I thought that perhaps what surprised me most about this life is how long it had taken to call it mine.

On a July night a few weeks after my meeting with Ron, I was driving to a friend's house for dinner when I realized that the burned ruins of the West Cummington Church were on the way. *You have time*, I told myself, as though time is what had kept me from Church Hill Road in those months since the fire. I turned and drove up the hill; I parked the car and walked to the great crater of rubble that was once the church. The stone steps remained intact, as did their black iron railing. I did not look closely at the ruins; I was not interested in what I might recognize, and regardless, anything recognizable had long since been salvaged. I sat down on the stone steps, right on the edge of that small sea of ash and stone and metal. I could have leaned over and touched it, but I kept my hands on the steps, which were warm from the sun.

It was a perfect summer night. The peepers were still calling; the creek was running fast enough to hear. The sky was the fading blue of a world surrendered to summer and its mist, its fecund haze. From where I sat on the steps I had a wider view of that place than I ever had before. There was no austere white church, no steepled bell tower to block the ledge that was now in view, wide and brown, blooming, water running down its face in sleek streams. I knew the ledge well from those Sunday mornings when June would not settle into sleep before the scripture reading and I would slip out the back door and walk along the ledge, shushing her to sleep. But it was always shadowed then, and I could never see more than the few feet of it in front of me. Now I could see the whole of it, washed in light.

22 | School Days

When Grace was in preschool, people often asked us where we were planning to send her to kindergarten. "Private school in Northampton," we would say. All the hilltown lesbians sent their kids there (the ones who didn't homeschool or win the lottery of the charter school) and so I answered without really thinking too much about it.

But when it actually came time for kindergarten we weren't so sure anymore. I had made peace with living in the hilltowns, and I didn't want Grace to go to school in town. I didn't want to spend so much of my life (and June's life) in the car. I enjoyed our days at home; I had good friends and a garden, favorite hiking trails, secret spots by the river. We spent much of our lives outside, in all seasons. Even June, who was only eighteen months old then, woke every morning and wanted to go outdoors, wanted to eat her breakfast under the pine tree while Grace did maintenance on yesterday's fairy house.

Chris was fine with the public school. She had never been as enthusiastic about private school as I had been. She worried about the social scene, and about the way it would limit her own involvement in Grace's school life, considering how far the private school was from her office. And while I was worried about public school, worried about testing and budget cuts and cafeteria food, I was also hopeful. Obama's first term wasn't even half over yet, and I was still buoyed by the activism and victories of his campaign and early presidency. I had volunteered for the campaign, and I still felt the sway of Yes We Can. I believed it would be worthwhile and satisfying to join our neighbors in making our little school a good one for all the town's children.

In the weeks before the 2008 election I had also been involved in the fight against Proposition 8 in California, staying up late to make phone calls and read position statements. And when Proposition 8 passed I organized a rally in support of marriage equality in the parking lot of the Creamery, our little hilltown grocery store and de facto community center. All our friends came. Greta wore Cyndy's wedding veil.

By the time Proposition 8 was threatening marriage equality in California, Chris and I had been legally married for four years. And legal marriage mattered. Now laws and social systems bore much of the responsibility for instructing people how to treat us, even those who didn't approve of our relationship. This was a powerful way to live, and it shaped the way we thought of ourselves as a couple. We wouldn't move to a state where gay marriage wasn't legal. We also knew that marriage equality was one of the reasons we could even consider sending Grace to public school.

Over the summer, I wrote Grace's kindergarten teacher a long letter explaining our family. "Grace has two moms," I wrote, "although she calls me 'Mom' and she calls Chris 'Mati,' so it will make the most sense to her if you also refer to us that way, as in, 'Did you go to New York with your Mom and Mati?'" I went on to explain that Grace had been conceived with the help of an anonymous sperm donor, which she knew, and that if any particularly precocious children asked about Grace's origins, the teacher could simply say we had help from a friend.

"Wow," Chris said, after she read the letter. "That's a lot of information."

"Better than not enough," I said, a little defensively.

"Absolutely," Chris said. She knew I was anxious. She handed me back the letter, pulled me toward her, and kissed my head. "Thanks for writing it."

In the weeks before school started, Grace's teacher-to-be held playgroups at the school playground to give the children a chance to meet each other and get to know her. I immediately liked Mrs. Patton; she was a slight and quiet woman with gray hair and thick, black glasses. She wore short skirts and clogs and pretty blouses, and she didn't ask the children questions she already knew the answer to. Because our friends' children mostly went to charter or private schools, Grace's kindergarten classmates were, for the most part, not children she had grown up playing with. They were the children of farmers and contractors, machinists, nurses. A few of them lived with their grandparents, and one was in foster care. There was a young scruffiness to her class that I both liked and was frightened by.

During the first weeks of school, Chris spent as much time at school as she could. She wanted the kids to see Grace's "other mom," and so she dropped Grace off a few mornings a week, helped her to unpack her backpack, and chatted with all the kids. At first they asked her who she was. "I'm Grace's other mom," she said. "She calls me Mati." Soon Grace's school friends began to call Chris Mati, as though it were her first name.

"Does that bother you?" we asked Grace. She told us she didn't mind. Chris, who had recently attended an Out and Equal conference panel with adult kids of gay parents, later told me that they had said not to believe your kid when she tells you something doesn't bother her. "They said she'll be trying to protect our feelings," Chris said.

"Those kids on the panel were old," I told Chris. "A totally different generation."

"It's not that different," Chris said.

This is how we seemed to have divided, how we covered all our bases: Chris worried about Grace's feelings about us; I worried about the world's feelings about her.

One evening in late fall, Mrs. Patton called me at home. There had been some discussion of marriage in the dramatic play area, she said, of who could marry whom. Most of the children were good with whatever, but a little boy had said, "Boys can't marry boys."

Mrs. Patton paused. I waited for her.

"And I know that this child comes from a religious family," she said slowly, "and so it felt a little tricky."

This is it, I thought. I tried to breathe. "Well," I said. "It's actually a fact, here in Massachusetts, that boys can marry boys. It's the law, regardless of what his family believes." Only later did the absurdity of the phrase "boys can marry boys" occur to me.

"Right," she said, "but families have such different beliefs." She spoke in the same warm voice I had heard her use with the children. As I listened to her I realized that in order to be a good kindergarten teacher you had to see the world in a way that I was far too self-righteous to see it.

"Well, it's not really about what his family believes," I said. "Gay marriage is legal in Massachusetts, and Grace's mothers are married. So she needs to hear you say that boys can marry boys. She needs to hear you say that you can marry whomever you love."

"You are right," Mrs. Patton said. "I hear you, and you are right. This is such a growing time for me. It's really amazing to stretch in this way."

Stretch on your own time! I wanted to scream. Figure it out! I couldn't believe that Chris and I had willingly put Grace in this situation. And why was her teacher calling me? Why wasn't she calling the parents of the little boy?

After I hung up the phone, I told Chris I thought we were sacrificing Grace to progress. "Calm down," she said. "She's hardly Amy Carter."

"We should send her somewhere where people know how to deal with this."

"Someone has to be the first," Chris said.

"Not Grace!"

"But why not, really?" Chris said. "I mean, she can handle it. And so can we. Besides, these kids are products of their environments. You can't fault them for what they say. They are parroting back what they hear from their parents."

"Somehow I don't find that comforting," I said.

I wanted to pull Grace out of school and send her to the Montessori school in Northampton. I wanted to spare her the burden of her difference. I wanted to spare myself. But here's the thing: I was also getting tired of trying to spare myself. I had been doing it for too long, and for what? The false promise of a life in which I kept it all—Catholicism, straight privilege, my marriage, and now, my children—yet paid no price, bore no loss? And in the meantime I had lost out on so much: my claim to a marvelous history, my place in an astonishingly powerful social movement, alliances with queer women who were poised to be dear and intimate friends. And all that desire.

For years I liked to say that Chris was the only woman I looked at, but this wasn't true. I looked at women all the time. And while I had colluded with the culture that says straight is the most desirable way to be, or at least to appear, I was beginning to acknowledge—and to enjoy—the fact that this simply wasn't true. I might not have been pushing any boundaries of gender identity myself—my hair was still long and layered, my bathroom cabinet filled with makeup—but I had long thrilled at the sight of people who were. Western Massachusetts was a lucky place to live not just because of the protections it offered but because of its queer culture, the gender-fluid students and baristas and parents who could make my day just by walking into it. For a long time I saw myself on the margins of this culture, as though I weren't gay enough to really count. But what did my own looks matter when the sight of a buzz cut and tattooed butch with a baby strapped to her chest was enough to stop my heart? It was my desire that made me gay enough, and always had.

My collusion was not only a personal denial but a political one. It had allowed me to ignore the responsibility I had to LGBT youth, people who needed to see me living out—all the way out—as a free and fulfilled adult. And as much as I wanted my daughters' world to be different, I could see now that it was even more important that the lives of young queers be different, that they see their futures clearly, claim their right to be beloved and content.

Which brought me back to the public school. Because what if a child in Grace's class—a rural, working-class child—was gay? And what if that child, on one of her dark days, remembered the sound of Chris's voice in the hallway, or the feeling of my coat brushing against her as I rushed in late, as I always did, and she remembered that we were gay and that we were also adults—autonomous and safe—and that thought allowed her to breathe into her future for a moment. This was bold of me, I know, to say that simply by existing I could be of any service. It wasn't enough, surely. But this was where I could begin, where we all can begin: by taking up our rightful space, by honestly and joyously occupying our bodies, our desires and beliefs, however we may choose to express them.

A few days after my conversation with Mrs. Patton, I decided to give her some books. I found every book I could about gay families and I bought them for the classroom. Or rather I called my parents and asked them if they wanted to buy all the books and donate them to Grace's classroom, which they immediately did. The day after I had given the books to the teacher, she told me she had read *King and King*, the story of a prince who wanted to marry a prince, and that a lively discussion had ensued. She told me she had loved every minute of it. "I'm on fire with this," she said. "We're going to blow it all wide open."

A Nest on the Altar 23

It took three years to rebuild the West Cummington Church. During those years of waiting and planning, services were held in the Parish House, a grand and slightly shabby white clapboard building adorned with Doric columns and a summer garden of echinacea and bee balm. Inside we sat on long, spindle-backed benches and metal chairs arranged in rows. The walls were painted a pale Edwardian yellow; the windows were trimmed in white. There were a few old oriental rugs on the floor and blueprints for the new church on the walls. I missed the old church, and I hardly ever went to Parish House services.

But in the year after I met Ron Ingalls I went a few times and felt a new weight. I felt it in my own body, and in my scattered but slowing mind, and I thought I heard it in Steve's sermons, in his voice. I know, certainly, that I saw it in his shoulders. It might have been the fire, or just aging, mine and his. But that was not all it was. I had a new glimmer of understanding that this tiny church was where God had planted me, and if I wanted to bloom, then I should pass some patient seasons here. I should start showing up to receive, without comparison, without fantasy. The task was to seal my heart to the God I found here. To look around and within, but to not look back.

One communion Sunday, Steve broke the round loaf of bread in half and handed it to the people on either side of him. "The molecules that are inside this bread," he said, "were once inside a star." He looked at the bread, and then looked around the room at all of us. "Is it the body of Christ?" he asked. He smiled, shook his head gently. "I don't know."

Steve's words rang inside me. Perhaps because of how he said them, part apology, part invitation. A doubt that did not move to diminish belief.

Is this the body of Christ? The plate had made its way around the circle to me and I took a piece of bread and held it in my hand while I waited for the others to take theirs. I didn't know either. But I loved it so.

The next week I told Chris that I was going to bring the girls to church. "Maybe they are old enough now," I said.

"Maybe," she said.

For a moment I thought of asking her if she wanted to come, but I knew she didn't. I was not bothered by her disinterest. She gave me West Cummington, all those years ago, and I was nothing but grateful, regardless of what the place might mean to her now. On Sunday morning when the girls and I put on our coats, Chris headed for the couch with the crossword puzzle. "Pray for me," she called as we walked out the door.

The girls and I arrived a bit late; we went in through the Parish House kitchen door and sat near the back with a bag of markers and paper, modeling clay, and juice boxes. Things went well that first Sunday, and so we went again the next week, and then the week after that. The girls were sometimes demanding, sometimes quiet. Grace always wanted to lay her head on my lap during the sermon, and controlling my annoyance at this was a spiritual exercise in itself. One Sunday, June made a small bird and nest from clay and put them on the altar during the offering. I joined a committee. I stayed for coffee hour and pretended not to notice how many cookies the girls ate. People stopped saying, "Oh, Erin, it's been so long," when I walked into the room. People stopped saying, "Look how these girls have grown."

Grace was eight and June nearly five when the new church was finished. It resembled the old church in many ways, but in many ways it did not, and people would talk about this for a long time. About what cannot be replicated. When I looked through pictures from the girls' baptisms I could see the old sanctuary's thin wainscoting, the red carpet, the simple sconces. I saw Steve's broader shoulders and my younger face. I saw my babies. I couldn't believe all that was once mine. I didn't miss anything or anyone so much as I was glad to have had it all. And glad for the luck of what had been returned to me: the sunlight through the tall windows, the view of apple trees, of the steep road down to the creek, and to the river beyond.

Secretly I wished for the new church to have a cross, even a small one, although I knew it never would. For years I had missed the cross at West Cummington. I wanted more cross; I wanted more Jesus. What I really wanted was my youth, the way it brimmed with possibility and all the time in the world. What I wanted was that brief Eden where I loved Chris but had not yet chosen her, when I still believed everything could be mine. But it couldn't. It can't. And so I have a church without a cross. "There is no cross at West Cummington," Steve said during one of the early sermons in the new sanctuary. He turned then and looked up at the bare wall behind him, the spot where a cross would hang if West Cummington were that sort of church. Instead there were white plaster walls, and a three-paned window framing a tower of pines outside.

"Crosses don't have much meaning for me," Steve continued. "I don't really find God in them. But many years ago a dear friend gave me a cross from a monastery in Vermont, and because I love this friend, I kept the cross. And when I go out into the woods to fell trees, I bring it. It hangs from a leather cord, and when I come to a tree whose lean I can't discern, I hang the cord from a low branch and let the cross plumb the line, tell me the tree's direction." He held up his hand, an invisible cord between his fingers. "The cross reminds me to give thanks for the tree, and to take my time in the woods."

Epilogue: Carol

In the winter of 2015, the film *Carol* came into wide release. *Carol* is based on the 1952 Patricia Highsmith novel *The Price of Salt* (later renamed *Carol*), which recounts the passion and torment of a love affair between Therese Belivet, a young and inexperienced shopgirl, and Carol Aird, a married woman with a child. The setting is midcentury New York and the affair is a dangerous one. Carol risks losing custody of her daughter to a vengeful and wounded ex-husband, and Therese, who has never loved a women before Carol, risks the end of security, the predictable future of a straight life.

Before I had the chance to see *Carol* I read all the criticism, listened to all the radio interviews. The mere existence of the film struck me as extraordinary—a Hollywood feature based on a book by a lesbian—and I loved all the press, and the buzz. I loved that the film was a queer endeavor: *Carol*'s screenplay was written by Phyllis Nagy, a lesbian playwright and friend of Patricia Highsmith, and the film was directed by Todd Haynes, a gay man.

Many of the articles I read referenced Highsmith's struggle to publish *The Price of Salt*. Her publisher passed on the manuscript, and it was later published under a pseudonym by a different house. These articles depicted Highsmith's publishing struggle as a tragic remnant of a distant past, as though bookstores were now chock-full of books about lesbians written by lesbians. As though even the well-read knew the name of any lesbian writer who was not Eileen Myles.

In the last week before the movie left town, Chris and I made a date to see it together in Amherst. We met there after work, in a bar across the street from the theater. This was what we did now that our children were older. We met each other in bars. We went on trips without the girls, spent nights in hotel rooms. Our daughters were eleven and eight years old. One of motherhood's greatest myths is the supposed bittersweetness of the children's aging. I have found it to be only sweet.

As the film began I indulged in the rare pleasure of deciding which member of the on-screen lesbian couple I most resembled. The last film that had given me the chance for this game was *The Kids Are All Right*, when after a few scenes I settled on the Julianne Moore character, right up until she has creepy bad sex with her sperm donor, at which point I decided I was a less uptight version of Annette Bening.

This time my alter ego was clear from the first moment. I was Thérèse Bellvet, the young shopgirl, the seduced. The one who can't quite believe what she wants, what she suddenly, absurdly, can't live without. It was pleasing to watch her move across the camera's dreamy Vaseline-smeared lens, both blurry and bright. She made me want to tame my hair and find my pearl earrings, buy a tweed skirt, order creamed spinach and eggs. She made me want to smoke.

I began to sour on the movie when Carol's husband leaves town with their daughter, threatening Carol with a child custody suit if she doesn't put a stop to her lesbian ways. This is a story line I detest: the woman who sacrifices motherhood at the altar of desire. I hate the story line because of my own telescopic and terrified response to it, which has always been: keep the child at all costs. As I watched, I thought, *Oh, Carol. Just don't. Go home, be quiet, keep secret. Have sex with your husband, tape up your marriage. What could matter more than your child?*

But then soon enough Carol and Therese are on the road, they are in a hotel room, and Carol's mouth is on Therese's body. And in that moment of watching them I knew what could matter more than anything or anyone else. I knew just as well as they did. So I was Therese, but I was also Carol. I was the girl who can't believe she wants it; I was the woman who will give up what she loves to keep it.

I had long kept my distance from the Carols of history, lesbians who lost everything to be themselves. I held them all at arm's length, preferring to think of my love affair as singular and apolitical, removed from time and even from my own identity, as though Chris were the only woman I would ever desire, the narrative of my sexual identity complete in the narrative of our sex. Kelly and her politics, Chris at the statehouse protesting the protestors—I had wanted to keep my distance even from the struggles of those closest to me.

But there I was sitting next to my wife—the woman with whom I had two children and a life insurance policy—watching a spectacle of harm and loss that I could not push away. Those women were my history, my foremothers. My life was built on the lives of women like Carol; my children existed because their children were taken from them and they refused to go home and keep the secret.

But that wasn't all. I watched the pained glances, the letter held too tightly, the phone receiver held too long. Carol's anxiety while she waits, broken, chastened, for a supervised visit with her daughter. Carol wasn't just my history. She wasn't just the before. I had more in common with Carol than I had, for so long, wanted to admit.

All those years ago I walked into a basement chapel and tasted the divine. I swam in deep waters of belief. For a time I was known and loved and home, and I believed great things would come to me. But what came to me instead was another desire just as profound, and entirely irreconcilable. The world I was born into was fuller than Carol's world but it was still broken.

Bit by bit I forged a new belief, and it was meaningful and complicated and real. But it wasn't better than the one I might have had if I had been allowed to remain a Catholic. I would have liked to do that. I would still like to. I would like a wider life; I would like to move through the world and claim anything that moves me, anything that expands my experience of being human. I would like not to be the person who watches a movie in which a woman loses her child and feels a kinship with that woman.

And yet. Carol's mouth on Therese's body.

I have known since I was twenty-four that I couldn't live without that. When I was a girl like Therese, a seed cracked in the fire of my wanting, and my whole life sprouted from it. It's funny to think of my life this way, passionate and urgent, destined. Surely it doesn't look it, here as a now forty-something woman with two children and a dog, a weedy garden, a mortgage. This is the life born of that fire! This life is essential and wild, the only possible life? Yes. Yes it is.

For years I was haunted by the shadow of the woman I thought I would become, the Catholic who crossed her children before they left for sleepaway camp, believing in the blessing and protection of her prayers, her sign. She was a second, impossible self, and she was maddening. But she's dear to me now. I no longer see her impossibility as a result of my weakness, my lack of faith, of determination. She's impossible because this world will not abide her, not yet. But I know her heart. I know what she believes.

On my office wall there is a photo of the Pantheon in Rome on Pentecost. In the photo countless blood-red rose petals are falling from the dome's oculus. The petals are a symbol, a dramatic reenactment of the first Pentecost when the Holy Spirit arrived as fire, igniting the apostles with the ability to speak in tongues that the people around them heard, and understood, in their own varied and native languages. Pentecost is the miracle that built the Church. In the photo, robed priests and worshippers reach for the petals. A child lies on the marble floor as though in a field, a red and fragrant sea. I hung the photo because I'm planning to go to Rome for Pentecost someday. I will stand under the Pantheon's domed ceiling, shoulder to shoulder with people of a faith that I love but can't claim, and I will wait for the petals to fall.

Acknowledgments

Thank you first to Heather Abel, editor and friend of my dreams, who urged me into the undiscovered country of memory and helped me make sense—and sentences—from what I found there. You made every page, and every day spent writing it, better.

I am deeply grateful to Joan Larkin for her early and sustained enthusiasm, and to all those at the University of Wisconsin Press who gave this book their time and attention, especially Raphael Kadushin, David Bergman, Amber Rose, Sheila Leary, Sheila McMahon, and Michelle Wing.

Rilla Askew and John Wideman taught me how to tell a story, and for that I can't thank them enough. Shauna Seliy, Brian Jordan, and the late Jim Foley offered marvelous camaraderie and still do, on earthly and astral planes.

Enormous gratitude to the West Cummington Church for being my home, and to Stephen Philbrick, who, to borrow his words, is a bright star in my shabby firmament. And thank you to Penny Schultz, for all the joy.

Rachel Jenkins gave me the room I needed, when I needed it. Erin O'Donnell, Karen Stevens, and Susan Warner took care of my girls so that I could write. Deborah Balmuth, Alisa Greenbacher, and Lori Shine read earlier drafts and responded with generosity and smarts. MB Caschetta and Cathi Hanauer made essential connections. Thank you all.

Thank you to Kelly Anderson for being family; to Cyndy Sperry for showing me how to be a mother and an artist; to Tim Davis and Susan Garsoe for a western desk; and Patsy Kauffman-Barber, Jen Nates, Alison Rogers, and Karin Wallestad for sustaining friendship.

And thanks to my family. The Corsacs brought me in with so much laughter and love. Thank you. Love and thanks to all the O'Neills and all the Whites, most especially to the world's best parents, Catherine and Jerry White, who filled deep wells of confidence and worth. And to my brother, Jerry, and sister, Rebecca, for faith and loyalty and for letting me have the middle seat in the VW bus. I would go anywhere with you two.

Grace and June, my darling girls, thank you for every last thing. I still can't believe you're mine.

Deepest thanks to Chris. Without you there is no story. Thank you for trusting me with it. Thank you for bringing it—and me—to life.

And one last debt of thanks: To the generations of LGBT people who wrote and spoke and marched, strategized and organized and testified and lay down in the streets so that I could have this life. Thank you. And thank you to the people who are still fighting, because the struggle is far from over. Thank you for your bravery and your vision. Thank you for being always on the side of love.

LIVING OUT

Gay and Lesbian Autobiographies

David Bergman, Joan Larkin, and Raphael Kadushin
FOUNDING EDITORS

The Other Mother: A Lesbian's Fight for Her Daughter
Nancy Abrams

An Underground Life: Memoirs of a Gay Jew in Nazi Berlin
Gad Beck

Gay American Autobiography: Writings from Whitman to Sedaris
Edited by David Bergman

Surviving Madness: A Therapist's Own Story
Betty Berzon

*You're Not from Around Here, Are You? A Lesbian
in Small-Town America*
Louise A. Blum

Just Married: Gay Marriage and the Expansion of Human Rights
Kevin Bourassa and Joe Varnell

Two Novels: "Development" and "Two Selves"
Bryher

The Hurry-Up Song: A Memoir of Losing My Brother
Clifford Chase

The Pox Lover: An Activist's Decade in New York and Paris
Anne-christine d'Adesky

In My Father's Arms: A Son's Story of Sexual Abuse
Walter A. de Milly III

Lawfully Wedded Husband: How My Gay Marriage
    Will Save the American Family
Joel Derfner

Midlife Queer: Autobiography of a Decade, 1971–1981
Martin Duberman

Self-Made Woman: A Memoir
Denise Chanterelle DuBois

The Black Penguin
Andrew Evans

The Man Who Would Marry Susan Sontag: And Other Intimate
    Literary Portraits of the Bohemian Era
Edward Field

Body, Remember: A Memoir
Kenny Fries

In the Province of the Gods
Kenny Fries

Travels in a Gay Nation: Portraits of LGBTQ Americans
Philip Gambone

Autobiography of My Hungers
Rigoberto González

*What Drowns the Flowers in Your Mouth: A Memoir
    of Brotherhood*
Rigoberto González

Widescreen Dreams: Growing Up Gay at the Movies
Patrick E. Horrigan

The End of Being Known: A Memoir
Michael Klein

Through the Door of Life: A Jewish Journey between Genders
Joy Ladin

*The Last Deployment: How a Gay, Hammer-Swinging Twentysomething
    Survived a Year in Iraq*
Bronson Lemer

Eminent Maricones: Arenas, Lorca, Puig, and Me
Jaime Manrique

Body Blows: Six Performances
Tim Miller

1001 Beds: Performances, Essays, and Travels
Tim Miller

Cleopatra's Wedding Present: Travels through Syria
Robert Tewdwr Moss

*Good Night, Beloved Comrade: The Letters of Denton Welch
    to Eric Oliver*
Edited and with an introduction by Daniel J. Murtaugh

Taboo
Boyer Rickel

Secret Places: My Life in New York and New Guinea
Tobias Schneebaum

Wild Man
Tobias Schneebaum

Sex Talks to Girls: A Memoir
Maureen Seaton

Treehab: Tales from My Natural, Wild Life
Bob Smith

Outbound: Finding a Man, Sailing an Ocean
William Storandt

Given Up for You: A Memoir of Love, Belonging, and Belief
Erin O. White